ENGLISH FURNITURE

FROM

CHARLES II to GEORGE II

English Edition limited to

one thousand five hundred copies

of which this is

No. **602**

First published London 1929
Reprinted 1980

© Copyright 1980 Mrs. Anne Courtin & Mrs. Virginia Evans
World copyright reserved
ISBN 0 902028 95 2

British Library CIP Data
Symonds, R.W.
  English furniture from Charles II to George II.
  1. Furniture, English — History
  I. Title   II. Antique Collectors' Club
  749.22   NK2529

Published for the Antique Collectors' Club
by the Antique Collectors' Club Ltd., Woodbridge, Suffolk

Printed in England by Baron Publishing, Woodbridge, Suffolk

WINGED ARM-CHAIR WITH MAHOGANY LEGS

Upholstered in the original fine stitch *petit-point* needlework

Circa 1735

ENGLISH FURNITURE

FROM

CHARLES II TO GEORGE II

A full account of the Design, Material and Quality
of Workmanship of Walnut and Mahogany
Furniture of this period; and of how
Spurious Specimens are made

BY

R. W. SYMONDS

With more than 260 Illustrations
from examples in the Collection of
PERCIVAL D. GRIFFITHS, F.S.A.

ANTIQUE COLLECTORS' CLUB

PUBLISHER'S INTRODUCTION

R.W. SYMONDS, who died in 1958, was rightly accepted in his lifetime as one of the greatest authorities on English furniture. While new discoveries have been made, new sources researched and additional knowledge come to light in the intervening years, nothing has happened to alter the importance of the contribution that Symonds made to the understanding of this subject. He has rightly been described as the first of the modern generation of scholars. This is clearly apparent in his approach to the subject; for him, as for the present day expert, detailed research and a close examination of the piece itself are what mattered. Thus this is one of the first books to illustrate, for example, such apparently humble but vital details as the screws used by cabinet-makers over a long period of time.

In re-presenting this fine book to a generation conditioned to handling books of lesser quality, mostly produced cheaply to achieve mass sales, it should be pointed out that the absence of the original photographs has inevitably slightly reduced the quality of the illustrations which in the original edition match any fine modern production. However the importance of the text and its relevance to the present day collector compensate for this small detraction from the original.

November 1980

R.W. Symonds, author of
'English Furniture from Charles II to George II'.

FOREWORD

I FIRST began to collect old furniture thirty years ago. At that date, furniture collectors were few and far between, and old furniture shops were correspondingly scarce. The wealthy collector in those days would have nothing to do with English furniture ; he interested himself in the more precious products of the Continent—in French furniture, *cinquecento* bronzes, Limoges enamels, and snuff boxes.

One outstanding peculiarity of this pre-war period of collecting was that walnut furniture was a drug on the market, and only oak, satinwood and mahogany were appreciated. Times have now changed, and it is walnut and mahogany that the present-day collector seeks for and admires. I must confess that I moved with the times, and consequently missed many an opportunity of acquiring magnificent pieces of walnut furniture when nobody wanted them, but which to-day are eagerly sought after, and are becoming increasingly scarce and correspondingly costly.

Walnut pieces that to-day run into four figures could have been easily purchased in 1910 for £80 or £100. This is no exaggeration, as I could name several examples of walnut furniture which were sold at Christie's at about that date and, on reappearing in the market in recent years, have realised more than ten times their original auction price.

The first piece of antique furniture that I ever bought was a mahogany bureau bookcase (illustrated fig. 131). I found it about thirty years ago when I was staying at an inn in Monmouthshire. The owner offered it to me for £40, and little did I think, at the time that I bought it, that this passing extravagance would inextricably involve me in the absorbing pursuit of collecting antique furniture.

In the first instance, the piece appealed to me as being extremely pleasing, and admirably designed as a writing desk. Its value in the furniture market was not a consideration that entered my mind, and I bought it purely because it satisfied my eye and suited my purpose. To-day, however, I look upon this piece from an entirely different standpoint. Its good proportions, its somewhat severe but excellent architectural design, the fine quality of the wood, and the excellent craftsmanship employed in its execution, have caused me to regard my first fine careless capture from a totally different point of view.

It is knowledge that leads to appreciation, and the fact that I bought this particular piece, instinctively perhaps, but in comparative ignorance, and have since learnt to understand and enjoy its real essential merits, confirms what the Author persistently advocates, that knowledge educates taste, and that taste develops through knowledge.

During the time that has elapsed since my original venture, I have passed through many vicissitudes in the pursuit of furniture collecting. For instance, after having collected furniture for five or six years, I was credited with having the finest collection of lion mask furniture in existence.

This unique distinction was short-lived ; for I soon discovered that the whole collection was spurious, and, what is more, had been made specially for me !

Undeterred by this set-back, I began again, with a considerably increased capital of knowledge—and an Agag tread—to resume my original intention which had been temporarily interrupted.

To-day, I consider this chapter of my experiences as a collector as a humorous interlude, especially when I happen to turn over the leaves of old art magazines and books, and find my spurious settees and chairs illustrated in all their borrowed splendour, and described in grandiloquent terms as masterpieces of eighteenth century cabinet-work.

I have a strong belief that to collect anything, and especially furniture, it is essential to set out with this point of view firmly in mind: that there is a world of difference between collecting and hoarding.

No collection can ever be perfect. The collector who knows this, and has the heart to part with one possession in order to acquire another, and does so deliberately and with discrimination, is still collecting, and is exercising his taste and his mind as well.

I also feel that the real collector is one who buys a piece, not for its utilitarian purpose but because it has intrinsic merit. Of course, one could carry this too far in a private collection, and acquire a superfluity of pieces of one *genre*, as, for example, a dozen sideboards or dining tables, all perfect of their kind, though difficult to dispose of in a house. But what I have done is to buy pieces of antique furniture which appealed to me as fine examples, and not allowed my choice to be influenced by pieces that happened to fulfil any required utilitarian purpose.

The danger of this form of collecting is that the collector is apt to turn his house into a museum; and yet, by a careful arrangement of one's furniture, and by avoiding over-crowding, one can still make a room habitable and comfortable, even if all the pieces in it are antique.

Some collectors attach considerable importance to securing what they consider to be bargains. From my past experience in collecting, I do not believe in bargains; that is to say, I do not believe in always trying to find the piece that one can buy, owing to the ignorance of the owner, at a very much lower price than its real value. The best bargains that I have ever made were in respect of pieces which I bought from the most important antique shops in London at the then market price, and which have ultimately turned out to be bargains, owing to the rise in value of the genuine piece. This is due to the greater competition between collectors who, possessing considerably more knowledge of furniture than they did previously, now recognise that a piece of good design and fine quality is desirable to possess. My advice therefore is not to buy a poor piece because it is cheap, but, rather, an expensive piece because it is good.

The tremendous interest that is taken to-day in old furniture is largely due to the extensive research work that has been carried out to discover exactly when and precisely how it was made. The question of construction, the consideration of the different varieties of wood, and the appraisement of design and quality are all matters that deeply interest and intrigue the present-day collector.

If this book had been published twenty years ago, it is probable that nobody would have either understood or even been interested in it, since the knowledge of the collector of those days was very superficial and scarcely went deeper than the classification of furniture into woods and periods.

This modern cultured and knowledgeable attitude towards old furniture I consider has been fostered, if not actually initiated, by Mr. R. W. Symonds.

It is for this reason that I welcomed his suggestion that he should illustrate this book with pieces of furniture in my own collection, especially as it is largely through his enthusiasm and great knowledge of what is best in old furniture that the collection has become what it is.

PERCIVAL D. GRIFFITHS.

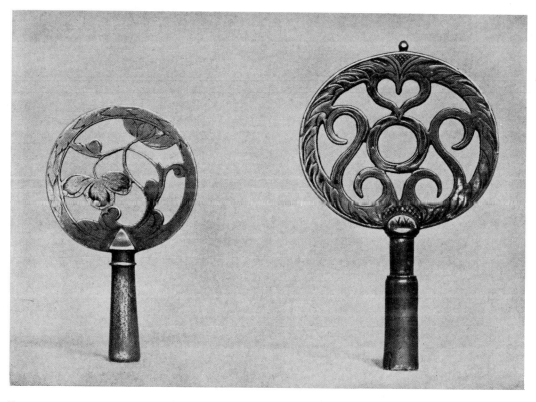

Fig. 1.—Late seventeenth century brass bracket clock keys.

PREFACE

IN my two previous books on the subject of old furniture, I described, to the best of my ability, the craft of the faker. My object was twofold, namely to expose him, and to prevent the collector from being imposed upon. Until these two publications, no one had ever seriously attempted to interfere with the faker's machinations, and he was thus left undisturbed to pursue the even tenor of his nefarious way. The revelations contained in my books produced a storm of indignation, and the strong winds of criticism were noisy about my head. This was only to be expected, and merely proved that some, at least, of my shafts had gone home. Incidentally, this critical outburst fully justifies the remarks made by Hogarth nearly two hundred years ago. "And whoever dares be bold enough to detect such impositions, finds himself immediately branded, and given out as one of low ideas, ignorant of the true sublime, self-conceited, envious ...."

I am moved to notice some of this criticism in that it has reached such a pitch of hysteria as to foster the allegation that I am myself a faker, and that my object in writing my books is to throw dust in the eyes of the collector. In this, my third book, it has seemed to me fitting to disclaim any such tortuous and ingenious motive. I have studied old furniture for over twenty years, and have endeavoured to learn about it from every possible aspect. The detection of fakes is a very fascinating pursuit ; and the knowledge that I have gained in it leads me to proclaim myself the sworn enemy of the faker, and, for want of a better title, an exposer of fakes.

In this book I have expounded certain theories with regard to furniture that are not in agreement with my previous books. For instance, I here maintain that veneered walnut and marquetry furniture was made in the first decade of Charles II's reign. In my previous books I placed the date of the manufacture of this furniture not earlier than 1675. I have also amended my remarks on early dovetailing, and on the first use of cock beads to drawers.

I am deeply indebted to Mr. Percival D. Griffiths, F.S.A., for allowing me to illustrate this book with the beautiful furniture in his collection, as, not only does it aptly illustrate the theories I have put forward, but the whole series of photographs will, I feel, be of considerable value in the education and training of the eye of the student, as regards those two important factors—design and quality.

In this collection, each piece is representative of the best work of the English cabinet-maker from 1660-1760, to which period Mr. Griffiths has confined his activities, and it contains no piece of exotic design, foreign to the tradition of that epoch.

Mr. Griffiths' criterion has been good design, fine quality and original condition. No higher standard could any collector set himself to maintain.

I have also to thank Mr. John C. Rogers, A.R.I.B.A., for the great trouble and care he has taken in preparing the excellent drawings of constructional details and mouldings, and for the measured drawings of the fine walnut bureau bookcase. Lastly, I wish to thank Mr. E. F. Gibbs, of Messrs. Cooper & Humphreys, for the skill and care he has exercised in taking the photographs.

R. W. SYMONDS.

22, Cheyne Row,
     Chelsea,
        London.

February, 1929.

Fig. 2.—Detail showing fineness of execution of gesso work on gilt fire-screen, Fig. 234

CONTENTS

LIST OF SUBSCRIBERS

HER MOST GRACIOUS MAJESTY THE QUEEN.
HIS ROYAL HIGHNESS THE PRINCE OF WALES.
HER ROYAL HIGHNESS THE DUCHESS OF YORK.
HER HIGHNESS PRINCESS MARIE LOUISE.
THE RT. HON. THE VISCOUNT LASCELLES, K.G., D.S.O.

ACKROYD, MISS
ACTON SURGEY, LTD., MESSRS.
ALLEN, MESSRS. ALFRED
ANGELL, CHARLES, ESQ.
ANGUS & ROBERTSON, LTD., MESSRS.
ANSTEY, CHRISTOPHER, ESQ.
ARMSTRONG, HARRY, ESQ.
ART MOBILIER, L', BRUGES
ASH, GRAHAM BARON, ESQ.
ATHENÆUM CLUB, THE
ATKINS, HAROLD B., ESQ.

BAGUES, LTD., MESSRS.
BAIRD, DOUGLAS, ESQ., C.B.E.
BAKER, D'ARCY, ESQ.
BARON, MRS. LOUIS B.
BARON, MAURICE B., ESQ.
BARRYMORE, J. M., ESQ.
BATSFORD, HARRY, ESQ., Hon. A.R.I.B.A.
BATSFORD, LTD., MESSRS. B. T. (18 copies.)
BAXTER, MARTIN, ESQ.
BECTIVE, THE RT. HON. THE EARL OF
BEETON, H. R., ESQ.
BEHRENS, FREDERICK, ESQ.
BEIT, SIR OTTO, BART., K.C.M.G., F.R.S.
BELL-IRVING, MRS.
BENARDOUT, J., ESQ.
BENDIR, ARTHUR, ESQ.
BENJAMIN, E. H., ESQ.
BETHELL, THE HON. RICHARD
BETHNAL GREEN PUBLIC LIBRARIES. (J. Radcliffe, Esq.,
    Chief Librarian.)
BIANCO & SONS, MESSRS. D.
BIERER, AUGUST, ESQ.
BILTMORE HOTEL, NEW YORK
BLACKWELL, LTD., MESSRS. B. H.

BLACKWELL, GEOFFREY, ESQ.
BLAIRMAN & SONS, MESSRS. H.
BLOCK, FRANK I., ESQ.
BLUMBERG, MARCO, ESQ.
BONDY, RICHARD C., ESQ.
BOTIBOL, J. M., ESQ.
BOWMAN, J. McENTEE, ESQ.
BOWRING, CHARLES W., ESQ.
BOYD, MRS. CARLISLE
BRADSHAW, R., ESQ.
BRETT & SON, MESSRS. ARTHUR
BROAD, JOHN, ESQ.
BROOK, CLIVE, ESQ.
BROWETT, ERIC M., ESQ.
BROWN, HENRY J., ESQ.
BROWNLOW, THE RIGHT HON. LORD
BRUCE, W. T., ESQ.
BUMPUS, LTD., MESSRS. JOHN & EDWARD
BURGE, GEORGE S., ESQ.
BURLINGTON FINE ARTS CLUB, THE
BURRILL, MRS. MIDDLETON S.

CARNARVON, THE RT. HON. THE EARL OF
CARNARVON, THE RT. HON. THE COUNTESS OF
CARNARVON, ALMINA, COUNTESS OF
CARPENTER, B., ESQ.
CASTLE, L. O., ESQ.
CHAFY, H. E., ESQ.
CHARLES, C. J., ESQ.
CHARRINGTON, GUY, ESQ.
CHARRINGTON, MISS DORIS
CHERRY-GARRARD, APSLEY, ESQ.
CHICHESTER, JOHN REGINALD, ESQ.
CHRISTIE, MANSON & WOODS, MESSRS.
CLARK, BRIGADIER W. E.
CLARKE, A. W., ESQ.

CLARKE, C. B. O., ESQ.
CLIFFORD SMITH, H., ESQ., F.S.A.
COLONIAL WILLIAMSBURG, INC., MESSRS.
COLVILLE, THE LADY CYNTHIA
COLVILLE, CAPTAIN N. R.
COMMIN, JAMES G., ESQ.
CONNELL, DAVID, ESQ.
CONNELL & SONS, LTD., MESSRS. JAMES
COOPER & HUMPHREYS, MESSRS.
COPE, R., ESQ.
CORY-WRIGHT, SIR ARTHUR, BART.
CREAGH, J. R., ESQ.
CROWTHER & SON, MESSRS. T.
CUBITT, CHARLES CYRIL, ESQ.
CULL, MRS.
CURTIS, MISS FLORENCE L. C.

DANSKE KUNST INDUSTRI MUSEUM, COPENHAGEN
DEAKIN, CYRIL, ESQ.
DEAN, EDWARD, ESQ.
DEIGHTON-PATMORE, JOHN, ESQ.
DELMÉ-RADCLIFFE, RALPH, ESQ.
DEMETRIADI, G. C., ESQ.
DIGHTON, BASIL, ESQ.
DORMER, MRS. R. S.
DOWER HOUSE, LTD.
DRURY, F. S. E., ESQ.
DUNN, SIR JAMES H., BART.
DUVEEN, GEOFFREY, ESQ.
DUVEEN, JOHN, ESQ.

EATON & CO., LTD., MESSRS. T.
EDINBOROUGH, BERNARD, ESQ.
EDWARDS & SONS (of Regent Street), LTD., MESSRS.
EDWARDS, LTD., MESSRS. FRANCIS
EUMORFOPOULOS, G., ESQ.
EVANS, F. B., ESQ.
EVAN-THOMAS, LTD., MESSRS. OWEN
EYRE, WILLIAM, ESQ.

FABER, R. R., ESQ.
FALCK, HERR DIREKTOR HERMANN, DARMSTADT
FARINGDON, THE RT. HON. LORD, C.H.
FARMER, EDWARD, ESQ.
FARR, DANIEL, ESQ.
FARRELL, GEOFFREY, ESQ.

FASKALLY, PETER BLECK, ESQ.
FOYLE, LTD., MESSRS. W. & G.
FRANCIS, ROBERT TALCOTT, ESQ.
FRANK, ROBERT, ESQ.
FRANKLIN, MRS. W. B.
FRASER, MAJOR FORBES, M.C.
FRITZE, HERR C. E.
FROWENFIELD, MRS. WALTER
FRY, T. W., ESQ., F.S.A.

GALLOWAY, THE RT. HON. THE EARL OF
GALLOWAY, THE RT. HON. THE COUNTESS OF
GAMBURG, HUGO, ESQ.
GAPE, ERNEST JAMES, ESQ.
GARDENER, JOHN, ESQ.
GARVAN, FRANCIS P., ESQ.
GAVIN, BULKELEY, ESQ.
GIBBONS, MRS. J. H.
GILBERT, MISS DAVIES
GILL & REIGATE, LTD., MESSRS.
GILLOW & CO., MESSRS.
GINZKEY, MONSIEUR WILLY, MAFFERSDORF, CZECHO-
    SLOVAKIA
GLADWIN-ERRINGTON, G., ESQ.
GORDON & GOTCH, LTD., MESSRS.
GOSSLER, MRS. PHILIP G.
GRAHAM, E. R., ESQ.
GRAYSON, DENYS, ESQ.
GREEN & HATFIELD, MESSRS.
GRIFFITHS, GEORGE A., ESQ.
GRIFFITHS, GERALD C., ESQ.
GRIFFITHS, MISS
GRIFFITHS, MRS. GERTRUDE T.
GRIFFITHS, PERCIVAL D., ESQ., F.S.A.
GRIFFITHS, VINE, ESQ.
GUEDALLA, F. M., ESQ.
GUNDY, MRS. J. H.
GUTMANN, PAUL, ESQ.
GUY-PELL, WILLIAM, ESQ.

HAMILTON, G. C. HANS, ESQ.
HAMOND-GRAEME, LADY
HANNEFORD-SMITH, W., ESQ., F.R.S.E., Hon. A.R.I.B.A.
HANNEN, GORDON, ESQ.
HARRIS, LIONEL, ESQ.
HARRIS & SONS, MESSRS. M. (2 copies.)
HARRISON, MAJOR J. F.
HARRODS, LTD., MESSRS. (6 copies.)

MELCHETT, THE RT. HON. LORD, P.C., HON. LL.D.,
    HON. D.SC., F.R.S.
MELVILL, HARRY, ESQ.
METCALFE, THE LADY ALEXANDRA
MILLAR, CECIL, ESQ.
MILNER, THE RT. HON. SIR FREDERICK, BART., P.C.,
    J.P., D.L.
MITCHELL, MAJOR CHARLES
MOLLISON, WILLIAM, ESQ.
MORGAN, SIR H. E., K.B.E.
MORTIMER, ROGER, ESQ.
MORTON, HAROLD TRESTRAIL, ESQ.
MOUNT EDGCUMBE, THE RT. HON. THE COUNTESS OF
MOYES, EUSTACE, ESQ.
MULVILLE, W. M., ESQ.

NAST, CONDÉ, ESQ.
NEUMANN, LADY
NEW YORK PUBLIC LIBRARY, THE
NIDDRIE, GEORGE O., ESQ.
NOBLE, FRANK G., ESQ.
NUTTALL, W. E., ESQ.

ORR, WILLIAM J., ESQ.
OSBORNE & CO., LTD., MESSRS.
OSBORNE, CHARLES GLIDDEN, ESQ.

PALMER & WAUMSLEY, MESSRS.
PALMER, RUSSELL, ESQ.
PALMER, W. E., ESQ.
PARKER, LTD., MESSRS. A. H.
PARKER, OLIVER, ESQ.
PARTRIDGE, FRANK, ESQ., LONDON
PARTRIDGE, FRANK, ESQ., NEW YORK
PARTRIDGE, LEO., ESQ.
PARTRIDGE, LEONARD, ESQ.
PEMBERY, ALFRED C., ESQ.
PHILADELPHIA, THE FREE LIBRARY OF. (George S.
    Pepper Fund.)
PHILLIPS, PHILIP A. S., ESQ.
PILLING, J. A., ESQ.
PIPON, MRS. P. J. G.
PIXLEY, COLONEL FRANCIS W., V.D., F.S.A.
PLENDER, SIR WILLIAM, BART., G.B.E., HON. LL.D.,
    D.L., J.P.
POLLAK, J. A., ESQ.
PORTARLINGTON, THE RT. HON. THE COUNTESS OF

PRATT, MESSRS. C. J.
PRATT, SON & SONS, MESSRS.
PRESTIGE, MAJOR SIR JOHN
PRINGLE, MAJOR W. G., M.C.

QUARITCH, LTD., MESSRS. BERNARD. (2 copies.)

RAMSAY, MRS.
RANDALL, N., ESQ.
RAPHAEL, C. F., ESQ.
RAPHAEL, E. G., ESQ.
RAVENSDALE, THE RT. HON. THE BARONESS
READ, A. B., ESQ.
READ, HENRY, ESQ.
RECKITT, SIR HAROLD, BART., LL.B., J.P.
RENNIE, MISS LOUISE
RESOR, MRS. STANLEY
REYNOLDS, HARRY, ESQ.
RICE & CHRISTY, LTD., MESSRS.
RICHARDSON & GILL, MESSRS.
RICHARDSON, H., ESQ.
RICHARDSON, H. F., ESQ.
RIDLEY, THE RT. HON. THE VISCOUNT
RIDPATH, E. G., ESQ.
ROBERSONS, LTD., MESSRS.
ROBERTS, C. LANE, ESQ.
ROBERTSON, MISS D. A.
ROBINSON, MRS. BEVERLEY, PARIS
RODRIGUEZ, MONSIEUR L., BRUGES
ROGERS, JOHN C., ESQ., A.R.I.B.A.
ROTCH, C. D., ESQ.
ROTHSCHILD, MRS. JAMES DE
ROUVROY, MONSIEUR MICHEL E. M., BRUSSELS
RUSSELL, ANDREW, ESQ.
RUSSELL, CHARLES E., ESQ.
RUTLAND, HIS GRACE THE DUKE OF
RYAN, SIR GERALD H., BART.

SACKVILLE, THE DOWAGER LADY
SALISBURY, THE MOST HON. THE MARQUESS OF, K.G.,
    P.C., G.C.V.O., C.B.
SALTMARSH, SIR GEORGE
SASSOON, MAJOR SIR PHILIP, BART., G.B.E., C.M.G.
SAWYER, LTD., MESSRS. CHARLES J. (4 copies.)
SCARSDALE, THE RT. HON. THE VISCOUNT
SCHMITT BROTHERS, INC., MESSRS.
SCHOLDER, MONSIEUR E., BRUSSELS

Scott, Lindley, Esq.
Severne, Captain E. C.
Shoreditch Public Libraries. (Thomas Green, Esq.,
     Librarian.)
Simmons, Harry, Esq.
Sinclair, Henry M., Esq.
Sligo, The Most Hon. The Marquess of, F.S.A.
Slomann, Herr Wilhelm von, Copenhagen
Smiley, C. H. Kerr, Esq.
Smith, A. Rae, Esq.
Smith, H. Sutcliffe, Esq.
Smith, R. Freeman, Esq.
Smith, Vivian Hugh, Esq. (2 copies.)
Sopwith, The Hon. Mrs.
Sotheran, Ltd., Messrs. Henry. (2 copies.)
Spanish Art Gallery, The
Spencer, The Rt. Hon. The Earl
Spencer, A. H., Esq.
Spier, Mrs. J.
Spink & Son, Ltd., Messrs.
Springate, George W., Esq.
Staal & Sons, Messrs.
Stair & Andrew, Ltd., Messrs.
Stationery Office, His Majesty's
Sterry, Sir Wasey, C.B.E.
Stevens & Brown, Ltd., Messrs. (9 copies.)
Stewart & Brown, Messrs.
Stoner & Evans, Messrs.
Story, Philip J., Esq.
Streletskie, Herr Henry, Stockholm
Swan, Esq., A. W.

Tabor, Major Sidney
Taylor, Joseph Dean, Esq.
Taylor, Myron C., Esq. (New York)
Taylor, W. Emuss, Esq.
Thompson, Henry Walker, Esq.
Thornton-Smith, Ernest, Esq.
Thornton-Smith, Ltd., Messrs.
Thursby-Pelham, James, Esq.
Tibbenham, Frederick, Esq.
Tibbenham, Messrs. Frederick
Times Book Club, The
Tinker, Edward L., Esq.
Tiranti & Co., Messrs. John
Toulmin, Mrs. H. W.
Townsend, Mrs. Edward M.
Tozer, Messrs. D. Charles

Trollope, Fabian G., Esq., C.B.E.
Trotter, Colonel Charles, C.B.
Truslove & Hanson, Messrs., Clifford Street
     (3 copies.)
Turner, Cecil F., Esq.

Urquhart, Leslie, Esq.

van der Woude, Mrs. R.
van Winsun, J., Esq.
Vernay, Arthur S., Esq.
Victoria and Albert Museum Library, The
Victoria Art Galleries and Municipal Libraries,
     Bath

Warde-Aldam, Mrs. W. W., M.B.E., A.R.R.C.
Waring, The Rt. Hon. Lord
Waring & Gillow, Ltd., Messrs., London
Waring & Gillow, Ltd., Messrs., Brussels
Warner, Miss Mabel
Webster, Percy, Esq.
Weissberger, H. P., Esq., Madeira
Wendell, Arthur R., Esq.
Wendell, Mrs. Barrett
Wendell, Mrs. Barrett, Jun.
Wendell, Mrs. Jack
Wendell, Mrs. M. F.
Wernher, Colonel H. A.
Westminster City Libraries. (R. B. Wood, Esq.,
     Librarian.)
Wiese, Fernando, Esq., Lima
Wiggins-Davies, W. T., Esq.
Willeby, Charles, Esq.
Williams, S., Esq.
Williams, Sidney J., Esq.
Williams, William, Esq.
Williamson & Sons, Messrs. W.
Willoughby, Brigadier-General the Hon. Charles
     S. H. D., C.B., C.M.G.
Willson, Walter H., Esq.
Wilson-Filmer, Mrs.
Winterbottom, Mrs.
Woodall, Corbett W., Esq.
Woodall, Henry, Esq. (2 copies.)

Young, Howard J., Esq.

CHAIR WITH ORIGINAL NEEDLEWORK COVERING

Legs of Sabicu wood, with enrichment gilt

Circa 1735

CHAPTER I.

GENERAL PRINCIPLES

THE beauty of old English furniture lies in the manner in which it truly reflects the character, outlook and habits of the people who designed it, made it and used it. It was made in various styles which followed one another in the true transitional manner, each succeeding style owing something of its inspiration to that which preceded it.

A style is the modification of design by the spirit of the period to which it belongs. It is, as it were, the concrete expression of a people's disposition and temperament, and, as long as it remains faithful in this respect, it continues in favour. For a style to be good it must have marked characteristics peculiar to itself, and must be founded on principles of artistic truth. This was particularly so as regards the great and acknowledged styles of the past, which were essentially a reflection of the ideals of the races to whom they owed their origin. Furniture has still more closely reflected the changing habits of succeeding generations, by reason of its near relation to the domestic requirements of the community. For example, with the accession of Charles II. to the throne, there arose a society which spent money more freely than under the Puritan Protectorate. It sought to recapture the spirit of long repressed gaiety, and foreign fashions and ideas were introduced from the Continent in order to meet a demand for novelty. In consequence, the change of conditions, new modes of life and ways of thinking affected all domestic usages, and were particularly reflected in the design of furniture. It was gay in character, as exemplified by the elaborate carving and turning of the chairs and the coloured marquetry of the cabinets, chests and clock cases. In the reigns of George I. and George II., furniture was solid and dignified. It no longer had the exuberance of design of late seventeenth century furniture. It reflected the settling down of Georgian England and the prosperity born of commercial enterprise. It was the furniture demanded by a methodical nation to whom comfort and culture were the necessary portion of the well-to-do. Women led sedentary lives, spent chiefly in playing cards and plying their needle. The strong architectural influence seen in bookcases and cabinets indicates the interest taken by the amateur in architecture. In the years between 1750 and 1770, a period of unrest, a renewed craze for novelty explains the introduction of French, Chinese and Gothic *motifs*. The design of eighteenth century furniture owed its most characteristic features to the influence of the wealthy classes. The less well-to-do used furniture of similar design, but simpler and plainer. The craftsmen's contribution consisted of a skill born of a tradition of hand labour and a slowness of execution made commercially possible by a small wage. Material also affected the design. The introduction of finely figured woods caused furniture to be veneered instead of being made in the solid ; and this treatment in turn affected the design of the furniture. The advent of mahogany for furniture permitted the use of wider planks of timber, which again resulted in a modification of design. All these and many other factors determined the styles of seventeenth and eighteenth century furniture.

Style should not be confused with design. It is the mode of presenting a design in any given period. Many different designs are contained within one style ; all are controlled in the manner of their presentation by the style to which they belong. In the Queen Anne and Victorian styles, use is made of similar *motifs* of design, but such *motifs* vary in manner and treatment in proportion to the greater differences between the two periods—differences of attitude, character and feeling. Their architects and designers employed the same classical *motifs* ; but with execution there came variation. Styles cannot be regarded as being in watertight compartments ; but, as they evolve one from another, so do they affect the design of everything in any given period. Buildings, decoration, furniture, silver, all these are co-related in design if they are of the same style. In addition, various materials tend also to influence the execution of design. A design executed in wood is not the same as one executed in stone, even though they are of the same style. It is the treatment which is different and not the design, as the same *motifs* may be carved in each. Each style has also its individual proportion—the proportion affecting the mass.

Appreciation is largely conditioned by knowledge. The knowledge and appreciation of old English furniture may be acquired in various ways. There is the study of style and design, which latter includes the appraisement of good and bad design. There is the study of quality in craftsmanship and methods of construction, with which must be coupled the whole question of quality and variety of materials used. Design is not dependent upon quality of workmanship or material ; whereas these last generally depend upon each other. A piece can be of good design, although roughly made by a country joiner from a coarse and cheap timber, such as elm. In the same way, a piece may be made by a highly skilled craftsman out of the finest materials and yet be bad in design. An axiom of the old cabinet-maker was that good craftsmanship demanded good material.

Design, however, is far the most essential quality by which to determine the æsthetic value of an old piece. In order to appreciate good design, the following principles, common to all styles, should be understood. A piece of furniture is in three dimensions—height, width and depth. The combination of these three forms the mass. Proportion is the mutual adjustment, not only of these dimensions, but of the various parts of the mass so as to produce a harmonious whole. The dimensions of the mass should be determined by the use for which the piece is intended, as fitness in this respect demands certain definite measurements. The height of a chair seat and a table top, and the length of a bed, should be functionally appropriate. William Hogarth, in his *Analysis of Beauty*, writes : " The bulks and proportions of objects are govern'd by fitness and propriety. It is this that has establish'd the size and proportions of chairs, tables, and all sorts of utensils and furniture." The relation of fitness to purpose was always borne in mind by the old furniture designers, and it is undoubtedly due to their close adherence to this principle that the design of old English furniture is of so high a standard. Hogarth, writing further on this subject, remarks : " Whatever appears to be fit, and proper to answer great purposes, ever satisfies the mind, and pleases on that account."

FIG. 3.—MIRROR WITH FRAME OF STUMP NEEDLEWORK ENCLOSED BY TORTOISESHELL MOULDINGS.   CIRCA 1665.
THE FULL LENGTH FIGURES REPRESENT CHARLES II AND CATHARINE OF BRAGANZA.

5

FIG. 4.—TOILET MIRROR WITH FRAME OF STUMP NEEDLEWORK ENCLOSED IN TORTOISESHELL MOULDINGS.   THIS MIRROR IS BRAIDED ON THE BACK WITH THE INITIALS A.P. AND THE DATE 1672 ; IT ORIGINALLY HAD A STRUT ON THE BACK SO THAT IT COULD STAND ON A TABLE. THE ORIGINAL OAK TRAVELLING CASE BELONGING TO IT STILL EXISTS.

6

Construction is also controlled by fitness, and constructional lines should not be obscured but left evident. In other words, they should not be distorted for reasons of decoration, so as to impair their purpose and fitness. Victorian furniture of extreme rococo character in the Louis XV. style is an apt example of such distortion carried out to the detriment of the design. Constructional lines should "carry through." In a piece composed of two parts, such as a bookcase, if the lower part is designed with a break front, then the upper part should have a break front also. This endows the two parts with a unity of design occasioned by the vertical lines of the projecting portion running the entire height of the piece.

Unity, as a factor of design, is again of the utmost importance. Every part of a piece should be in sympathy with the others and with the whole. Should any part of a piece which is governed by this principle be removed, the remaining parts will appear incomplete, since every part, if the whole is of good design, has its significance, and the removal of any one will impair the rest. Thus the trained eye will immediately detect the absence from a piece of furniture of any portion which, through misuse and neglect, has been damaged or removed. The cutting off of the domes from the hoods of long-case clocks, in order to permit them to be placed in a low room, may be cited as an example of this. It will be immediately noticed that the design is incomplete. Additions will also be obvious. For instance, in the case of a chair which was originally designed as a single chair and has had arms added, thus converting it into an armchair, the arms will not be in strict harmony with the back and legs. It was never intended that the chair should have arms, and their addition will destroy the proportions inherent in the original design.

Another important defect in design may be detected by the discerning eye trained to appreciate unity, when a piece has had a missing portion replaced, such as the stem of a tripod table to which a new top has been fixed. If the table was originally of good design, the dimensions of the top and base would stand in such proportionate relation to one another as to give a sense of unity to the whole. A top that is too large or too small for the base will err in this respect. Or again, when a chest on a stand has had a new stand made for it, the original one being missing, it should be at once possible to decide whether the modern stand is in fair proportion to the chest, and the whole possesses unity of design. Proportion should be definite and decisive. A bookcase 8 feet high, with the lower part 2 feet high, is of far more pleasing and decisive proportions than if the lower part were 3 feet 6 inches and the upper part 4 feet 6 inches.

Ornament is subordinate to structure. It should emphasise the lines of structure, and not obscure or deflect them. Ornament, if it is to realise its fullest decorative value, must be imposed upon a plain background. Over-ornamentation defeats its own end. The eye can properly appreciate ornament only when it is in contrast to a plain surface. Plain mouldings are ornamental in themselves. Mouldings seen in elevation are only noticeable by their shadows. Ornament and mouldings should be as much in scale with the piece they decorate as with each other, and should be in harmony of treatment and style.

That seventeenth and eighteenth century furniture was of a high level of design and of excellent proportions is undoubtedly due to the close adherence to the principles of classical architecture. Thomas Chippendale, in the preface to his *Director*, asserts : " Of all the arts which are either improved or ornamented by Architecture, that of cabinet-making is not only the most useful and ornamental, but capable of receiving as great assistance from it as any whatever." Not only did the old designers base the proportion of their pieces upon the classical orders, but they copied the sections of mouldings, and in many cases derived their ornament from classical examples. This close adherence in furniture design to architectural principles was specially prevalent in the first three-quarters of the eighteenth century, and particularly noticeable in such pieces as bookcases and cabinets. Designers in this period sometimes carried the adoption of architectural treatment to the absurd length of combining a bookcase with a structure of classical proportions with Chinese and Gothic *motifs*.

Chippendale gives in his *Director* the design of a winged bookcase of classical proportions with a surbase and plinth. The traceries of the doors are composed of pointed ogee Gothic arches, and the cornice consists of a parapet pierced with quatrefoils surmounted with Gothic finials. Such a bookcase is made in defiance of those principles of design which demand that ornament and structure should be in harmony. Gothic ornament should only decorate a structure which is Gothic both in proportion and character, these being as peculiar to it as are classical proportion and character to a classical structure. A fundamental error of design such as Chippendale's would pass unnoticed by an untrained observer. Many people, who are otherwise fully conversant with the various styles of old furniture, are quite unable to recognise good from bad design in individual pieces, as both their mind and eye are entirely untutored in this respect. Knowledge of styles can be learnt from text-books ; but appreciation of the intricacies of design requires, not only knowledge of its principles, but the constant instruction of the eye by means of the examination and analysis of many thousands of pieces of furniture. Such understanding presupposes a sensibility which not everybody owns. Those endowed with this faculty will soon be able, once they have obtained a general knowledge of first principles, to recognise good and bad design at sight, even if they are yet unable to analyse their impressions. Other less fortunate people, who are without this instinct, will still be unable after years of constant training to appraise good design correctly. The essential importance of a knowledge of design to the student and collector lies in the fact that old furniture is very far from being always of good design ; indeed, it may be said that much of it is extremely poor, and therefore, from an æsthetic point of view, valueless, no matter how fine the craftsmanship or how good the material. This æsthetic value should control the monetary worth of old furniture to-day, and that it does not always do so, apart from the indiscriminate cult of the antique, is because design is not generally understood, and therefore not appreciated. To many people good design in furniture is confused with the amount and quality of ornament. If a piece possesses elaborate and florid ornament, then it is supposed to be desirable and commercially valuable. This utterly mistaken attitude has arisen largely by reason of the attraction which ornament possesses

FIG. 5.—CHIMNEY GLASS WITH BEVELLED GLASS BORDERS CONTAINED IN CARVED GILT MOULDING.　C. 1695.
MIRRORS OF THIS DESCRIPTION WERE ESPECIALLY DESIGNED TO GO OVER A CHIMNEY-PIECE,
USUALLY WITH A MARBLE BOLECTION SURROUND AS SHOWN.

Fig. 6.—MIRROR WITH GILT GESSO FRAME WITH CRESTING SURMOUNTED BY A COAT OF ARMS.   CIRCA 1710.
THIS MIRROR IS ONE OF A PAIR.

for the untrained mind. Ornament is only one of the small factors of design, and the best design can exist without it.

Ornament should be used to relieve the severity of structure, and its proper and adequate employment requires considerable discernment on the part of the designer. Over-ornamented pieces which disregard the principles here referred to have survived in considerable quantities, especially mahogany examples dating from the middle of the eighteenth century. In such pieces the ornament is made to become a part of the structure. Chippendale, in his *Director*, gives designs for chairs with the splats of the backs composed of ribbons. The purpose of the splat in a chair is to support the back of the occupant. A bow of wooden ribbons may actually support a person's back, but it is an artistic heresy to fashion a silk ribbon in wood and make it fulfil a structural purpose, which, in the material it imitates, it could never do. The commercial value of ribbon-backed chairs of this description is considerable, as they are much prized by collectors, either because such furniture appears pretty or decorative to the uncultured eye, or, perhaps, because it is rare and may possibly have come from the extensive workshops of the famous Chippendale himself. The collector of this last and not uncommon type can know nothing of the pleasure which can be derived from looking at and possessing things of real intrinsic merit. The great proportion of sixteenth, seventeenth and eighteenth century English furniture has considerable æsthetic value. The failure to realise and appreciate this does little else but degrade it to the level of pot lids, or such-like meretricious objects of collection, which have no value artistically, and should therefore, by rights, have none commercially, unless it be a utilitarian one. An axiom that collectors would do well to remember is that an object, if it does not justify its presence in a room by virtue of its utility, should be artistically more valuable to the room than the space it occupies.

The student's knowledge and appreciation of design will add enormously to the collector's pleasure in the possession of old furniture, for it would neither be worth studying nor possessing if it were not for its artistic qualities. Given that a piece of furniture is of good design, there arises the question of appraising it on the basis of its craftsmanship and the quality of the material from which it is made. Quality is a far more comprehensive study than it would appear to be at first sight. The manner in which the dovetails have been made, the finish given to the drawer linings, the fineness with which the carved or inlaid ornament has been executed, the question of whether inferior or good quality woods were used for the carcase and drawer linings, whether the veneer used for the exterior is finely marked, or whether it is a plain unfigured veneer chosen for reasons of cost—all these considerations must be carefully assessed before judgment on the collective excellence of a piece is passed. In considering craftsmanship, it should first be realised that, throughout the three hundred years ending with the birth of the nineteenth century, the workmanship of the English cabinet-maker consisted of a gradual evolution of refinement. The period can be divided up into schools : the late Gothic, or early sixteenth century school ; the Elizabethan ; the Jacobean ; the Charles II. ; the William and Mary and Queen Anne ; the early mahogany and late walnut ; and the Adam and late eighteenth century schools. Not only was the quality of workmanship different in each school, but the methods of construction varied also throughout.   Naturally there was considerable overlapping both as regards design and manner of construction.   For example, in the reign of Charles II. the modish London cabinet-maker was turning out furniture in the modern style with up-to-date methods of construction and workmanship. The drawers were dovetailed with wide, coarse dovetails, and the piece, instead of being left in the solid wood, was veneered with walnut.   Furniture was also being produced, by smaller cabinet-makers, of oak in the Jacobean style, with the drawers, instead of being dovetailed, nailed and hung on runners fixed to the carcase, which fitted into grooves made in the drawer sides.   In the country districts, there were still joiners making furniture decorated with Elizabethan *motifs*, and even with a feeling of Gothic design. At this period, as also in the eighteenth century, design and new methods of construction were but slowly assimilated in the country districts.   In the time of George I., while the cabinet-maker in London and the large provincial towns was constructing furniture in walnut, with cabriole legs to his chairs, his country *confrère* was making chairs of oak with turned legs in the Jacobean style.   This overlapping of styles, use of material and methods of construction is very confusing to the student, who requires considerable know-ledge of country-made furniture before he can assign with certainty the date of any given piece.

Again, in considering craftsmanship, it must be remembered that each individual school has various grades.   There was the first grade, to which the best and most costly furniture belonged.   This furniture was made out of the wood in vogue at the time.   In the Gothic, Elizabethan and Jacobean schools oak was employed ; from the time of Charles II. to Queen Anne, walnut ; from George I. to the accession of George III., mahogany was used as well as walnut.   In the Adam and late eighteenth century schools, mahogany and satinwood were principally employed.   Throughout these three centuries, inferior furniture was made of such woods as beech, chestnut, ash, elm and fruitwood ; while, in the eighteenth century it was also made of oak, which had by that time come to be considered a lower-grade wood.

Between the first grade of furniture—made for the nobility and the wealthy out of the finest and best material, and decorated in a lavish manner with carving and inlay over which no expense was spared—and the purely utilitarian furniture—made for the use of the poorer classes, the artisan or apprentice in the towns, and the yeoman and small farmer in the country—there was a middle grade which was made for the well-to-do merchant class.   This type of furniture was plainer and simpler than the costly first-grade pieces, although made of the same wood, and the majority of furniture that has survived from the sixteenth and early seventeenth centuries is of this type.   The lower-grade furni-ture of beech, chestnut, elm and fruitwood, dating from these periods, is practically non-existent to-day, although a considerable quantity of it must have been made at the time.   Furniture of soft wood could not have survived the wear and tear of three or four centuries so well as that made of oak.   From the late seventeenth and eighteenth centuries, furniture in soft woods has survived in considerable quantities, and far more eighteenth century furniture belonging to the third grade is extant to-day than that of either the first or second grades of the same period.

Fig. 7.—WALNUT BUREAU DRESSING TABLE, 1 FT. 10½ IN. IN WIDTH.　　CIRCA 1725.　　THE DRAWER LININGS ARE OF VIRGINIA WALNUT AND THE FRONT IS VENEERED WITH FINELY FIGURED BURR WALNUT.　　THIS PIECE IS OF EXCEPTIONAL QUALITY CRAFTSMANSHIP AND FINE PROPORTIONS.

13

It must be possible for the student to recognise these different grades of quality in furniture. They were determined largely by questions of cost, each grade supplying a different class of society. The original cost of a piece of furniture may be said to govern its present-day value ; that is, granted its design is good. The characteristics of the three grades in the various schools of cabinet-making are not necessarily the same. A high-quality piece of Elizabethan oak furniture has an entirely different quality from that of a high-grade piece of Charles II. walnut furniture. This is because the art of cabinet-making progressed considerably between the reigns of Elizabeth and Charles II. The Elizabethan school of cabinet-makers not only used a different wood, but their methods of construction and the technique of the carving differed from those of the Charles II. school. Furthermore, the furniture of the latter period came to a great extent under foreign influence, and was also veneered instead of being made, as previously, in the solid. All these differences contributed to the distinct characters of the two schools. The quality of George I. walnut furniture differed considerably from that of Charles II. By this time the craftsmanship had gained refinement, the constructional work was better, and the veneering and the cross-grained mouldings were more skilfully executed.

When appraising the quality of furniture, however, there is no real justification for making invidious distinctions between the quality of cabinet work in the times of Charles II. and George I. The furniture of both periods varies in quality from the best to the poorest ; but, beyond this, they have nothing in common, and, in order to classify a piece of good or bad quality in any period, it must be assessed in comparison with contemporary pieces only. In judging the quality of furniture the following points must be considered separately :

(1) The quality of the wood of the carcase and of the drawer linings.
(2) The quality of the wood of the exterior, or the veneer.
(3) The quality of the workmanship employed in the construction of the carcase, and specially the drawers, if any.
(4) The quality of the carving, the inlay and marquetry work, the matching of the veneer, the execution of the mouldings, and the general cabinet work of the exterior.

More particular information will be given in later chapters on the lines of observation to be taken in reviewing the question of quality of craftsmanship and material as regards walnut and mahogany furniture under these four heads.

Methods of construction play as important a part as quality in the understanding of old furniture. Methods of construction, of course, are partly dependent upon quality, cheaper methods being employed to reduce the cost of making. An example of this is the nailing of drawer sides instead of dovetailing them. This applies, however, only to late seventeenth and eighteenth century furniture, as the majority of the seventeenth century drawers of even the best quality were nailed together instead of being dovetailed. Alterations in methods of construction were principally due to new and better methods being invented, in the same way as quality of workmanship gained refinement with the passage of time.

c

The last and remaining consideration is that of the colour and surface condition of the wood, which is known as patina. The patina of a piece plays a very important part in the present-day appreciation of old furniture, and quite rightly so, for this quality can only be bestowed upon a piece by time. Many pieces have inherited a patinated surface, while many others are without it. Its presence on a piece endows it with an artistic merit and one that is inimitable, since it can only be produced by natural means—by long exposure to the atmosphere, bleaching by the sun, and the rubbing, polishing, dusting, touching and handling of generations during its many years of usage. The imprint of age upon an object confers upon it a quality of beauty all its own. This is true of buildings weathered by the elements, of bronzes oxydised by long exposure, of pictures mellowed by time, of tapestries faded by light, and of marbles bleached by the sun.

The principal effect of age upon the surface of furniture is the alteration of the colour of the wood, and, in a lesser degree, the effect that wear, usage and domestic polishing have had upon the surface during the lifetime of the piece. The colour of the wood changes gradually and imperceptibly by exposure to light. Walnut, deal, mahogany, pine and satinwood all darken with age. The change in the colour of the wood is, to a greater or less degree, dependent upon the alteration in the colour of the polish through exposure to the atmosphere and light. The extent to which this affects walnut and mahogany furniture will be discussed more fully in the chapters on the furniture made of these woods.

The beeswaxing and rubbing that a piece in domestic use has received since it was made have resulted, in many cases of oak and mahogany furniture, in giving the surface a bronze-like finish. A particular feature of the effect of patination on the carved ornament of oak, walnut and mahogany furniture, is the decorative effect obtained by ornament thrown into relief through the raised portions being lighter in tone than the background and interstices. These prominent parts of the carving, owing to their exposed position, will have received more domestic rubbing and polishing than those protected portions which have escaped the duster. In course of time, beeswax will have accumulated in these parts. Dust and dirt will have darkened the beeswax, which in time has solidified and itself become patinated. This accentuates the carved ornament, and gives it a quality of richness which it lacked when the piece was first made. Mouldings are also affected in the same manner. Unfortunately, as has already been stated, many pieces of old furniture have not these desirable attributes of patina. This is due to the fact that such pieces were repolished in the Victorian period. At this time a new type of polish came into fashion, known as French polish. It differed entirely from the spirit varnish, oil and wax polishes of the seventeenth and eighteenth centuries, whose application required much labour and time.

French polishing was a far shorter process, resulting in a high glass-like finish, which remained as a film on the surface of the wood. Such a polish appealed to the Victorian mind, and resulted in the ruination of many tens of thousands of pieces of seventeenth and eighteenth century English furniture, which were ruthlessly stripped of their patina, preparatory to being renovated and " finished " with this surface. It was indeed an unfortunate day when the Victorians discovered French polish ; for it not only destroys the patina and obscures the natural beauty and figure of the wood, but also disturbs the appearance of the piece owing to the reflections created by its mirror-like surface.

With patina, a catalogue of the many attributes of old English furniture is completed ; and in the following chapters it is hoped that the student and collector will find sufficient information to enable them to acquire a fuller understanding of walnut and mahogany furniture in particular. Such an understanding must be based on a knowledge of style, of the principles of design, quality of material and quality of craftsmanship, of the manner of construction, and of the patina of the surface attributable to the accidents of age.

FIG. 8.—MAHOGANY BRASS-BOUND WINE COOLER ON STAND WITH LEGS OF UNUSUAL DESIGN.   CIRCA 1750.

CHAPTER II.

WALNUT FURNITURE
1660-1760

THE walnut period of furniture in England covers approximately a hundred years. Walnut came into fashion about 1660, and from this date until about 1730 it was the popular wood for the furniture of both the wealthy and the middle classes. After 1730 mahogany began to compete with walnut, and, from then onwards, the best and finest pieces of furniture were made from the former wood. After 1750 the popularity of walnut began to decline; while, after 1760, it went out of fashion altogether.

This must be regarded as a very general statement, as there was a considerable overlapping between the use of walnut and mahogany from 1730 onwards. Walnut continued to be employed by the provincial cabinet-makers much longer than by firms in London, and, similarly, many cabinet-makers in London may have retained a preference for walnut, and, in consequence, made their best and finest pieces from this wood. Customers with conservative tastes may also have been the cause of fine pieces being made in walnut as late as 1750-60, for if they preferred the walnut wood to the mahogany they may have given a special order for the making of a walnut piece. Thomas Sheraton, in his *Cabinet Dictionary*, published in 1803, mentions that walnut " was much in use for cabinet work about forty or fifty years since in England, but is now quite laid aside since the introduction of mahogany."

Although a great amount of walnut furniture has survived, undoubtedly a considerable quantity of it has been destroyed, and this destruction must be taken into consideration in order to arrive at a correct understanding of the furniture of the walnut period. Considerably more walnut furniture has perished than mahogany, and this can be attributed to the fact that it was made with a veneered surface on a soft wood carcase which was subject to the worm, and decorated with applied cross-grained mouldings glued on to a soft wood core. Consequently, this furniture was unable to withstand the wear and tear of use as well as the contemporary mahogany furniture which, together with the mouldings, was made in the solid wood. Walnut was therefore discarded and eventually destroyed in greater proportion. Thus, although there is still more walnut furniture in existence to-day than mahogany, made prior to 1760, the original numerical superiority of walnut over mahogany pieces has dwindled.

The destruction of so much walnut furniture and the diminished amount now extant have led to the belief to-day that after 1740 it ceased to be made, and that the contemporary mahogany pieces were made in much larger numbers in comparison with the walnut than was really the case.

Evidence of the popularity of walnut furniture in the middle of the eighteenth century is to be found in a sale catalogue of the contents of the town house in Cavendish Square

17

PAIR OF SCONCES IN WALNUT FRAMES
Containing panels of *petit-point* needlework
Circa 1720

18

Fig. 9.—MARBLE SLAB TABLE ON WALNUT FRAME.   CIRCA 1730.

19

of James, Duke of Chandos, which was sold on his death in 1746.   Although it is probable that only a small amount of the furniture in the house at the date of the sale was new, nevertheless it is valuable evidence of the manner in which a wealthy nobleman's house was furnished at that time.   Out of sixty-five lots in which the name of the wood of the particular piece of furniture concerned is mentioned, thirty-six are walnut, eleven mahogany, and eighteen Japan lac.*

One especially interesting fact is that of the thirty-six articles made of walnut that are mentioned, eight are bookcases, whilst no bookcase is included among the mahogany pieces.   One of the rarest pieces of walnut furniture to-day is the bookcase, and its present-day scarcity is undoubtedly due, not to the fact that they were made in small numbers, but that they were destroyed because they became shabby and dilapidated.   This was mainly caused by the soft carcase wood being attacked by the worm, which in time affected the veneer, and also by portions of the cross-grained mouldings becoming loose and dropping off.   Therefore, in the late eighteenth and early nineteenth centuries, when mahogany furniture was the vogue, it was not thought worth while to repair a walnut piece.   This is especially true of a bookcase, which could not very well be used for any other purpose except to hold books, unlike a chest-with-drawers or a tallboy which, even if shabby, could always be put to some use, if only in the servants' quarters.   This may account for the survival of so many dressing tables and tallboys.†

None of the bookcases in the Chandos sale realised a higher sum than £8 10s.   The fact that such small value was attached to walnut furniture in this period is another un-doubted proof that a large piece such as a bookcase, which had become shabby and knocked about and out of date as regards design, was considered in the late eighteenth and early nineteenth centuries as a white elephant, and was therefore got rid of and eventually destroyed.

The present-day rarity of the walnut marble-topped side-table also presents an analogous case to that of the walnut bookcase.   To-day, a walnut side-table, similar to example illustrated (fig. 9), is of the greatest rarity.   Yet, judging from the Chandos cata-logue, where five walnut side-tables with marble tops are mentioned, it would appear that numbers must have been made.   The largest of those mentioned measured 6 feet 10 inches wide by 2 feet 6 inches deep, and is described as " a long marble sideboard table on a walnut-tree frame."   The price it realised was £3 10s. od.

Each time a table with a heavy marble top such as this was moved, the weight of the top was liable to wrench and strain the structure of the table.   A walnut table with its frame made of soft wood and its frieze veneered with walnut, with cross-grained mould-ings, would not have stood this treatment so well as a mahogany table.   Hence the survival of many mahogany examples and the great scarcity of those of walnut.

---

* It is interesting to note that the lacquer examples outnumber the mahogany ; this would point to a very large destruction of the former, as lacquer furniture is extremely scarce to-day.   Chairs are especially rare, and two sets of six Japan lac are listed in the catalogue.   This is not surprising when it is considered that lacquer furniture was made of deal or beech, both of which were extremely susceptible to the attack of the worm.

† Other pieces of walnut that have survived in large numbers are the bureau bookcase—which may have been retained because of the utility of its bureau portion—the long-case clock and the card table.

The reasons given for the destruction of walnut bookcases and marble-topped side-tables go to show that, because a piece is scarce to-day, it is no proof that it was not originally made in considerable numbers

STYLE AND DESIGN.

In considering the walnut furniture that was made throughout the hundred years referred to, it is necessary to divide the period into two definite styles, the first of which, dating from 1660-90, may be designated the Stuart style. The main characteristic of this style was that the constructional members were of a straight and not of a curvilinear form, which gave to the design a general feeling of rectangularity. The legs and uprights to the chairs were straight, and the stretchers and rails joined them at right angles. The same applies to the legs and stretchers of tables. The seats of chairs were straight-sided, and the sides and tops of cabinets and chests were straight and of rectilinear form without curved lines. Legs and stretchers of chairs and tables were spiral twisted or baluster turned. Carving was in high relief and pierced through. Parquetry and marquetry were used as media of decoration. This style was undoubtedly foreign, there being nothing characteristically English in it as regards design. It only differed from the foreign contemporary work by virtue of a typically English craftsmanship ; for, although he was copying, the English craftsman succeeded in endowing the design with the insular peculiarities born of the tradition in which he was working. No style in the history of English furniture had such an untraditional beginning as this Stuart style. In less than a decade the furniture altered not only in design and material, but also in construction ; and the unusual circumstances of the period must be considered in order to understand how this was possible.

A Puritan Commonwealth suddenly gave place to a popular monarchy and a Court. The social conditions thus re-established among the nobility and gentry created an urgent demand, among other things, for new furniture, which was as quickly supplied by the importation of foreign designs. Such designs were at once assimilated by the English craftsmen, and, although closely resembling the work of the French, Flemish and Dutch designers, were yet so stamped by English characteristics as to permit us, after a lapse of 260 years, to detect the differences between the two.

The next decade, from 1690-1700, which is known as the William and Mary period, was one of transition. It was a connecting link between the Stuart style and the style dating from 1700-60, for which, although Queen Anne's reign occupies the first fourteen years of the period, one can find no better name than the Georgian style of walnut furniture. Design in this style springs from an entirely different basis from that which preceded it. Instead of being rectangular it is curvilinear. The side rails and splats of chairs are curved ; the legs of chairs and tables are cabriole. The seat rails to chairs are curved, although at the end of the period they again become rectangular. The cornice mouldings to cabinets and bookcases have a deep hollow which in section is a curve. The tops of bureau cabinets, when not straight, are domed. The tops of doors of such cabinets are curved, and long-case clocks have their hoods surmounted by domes.

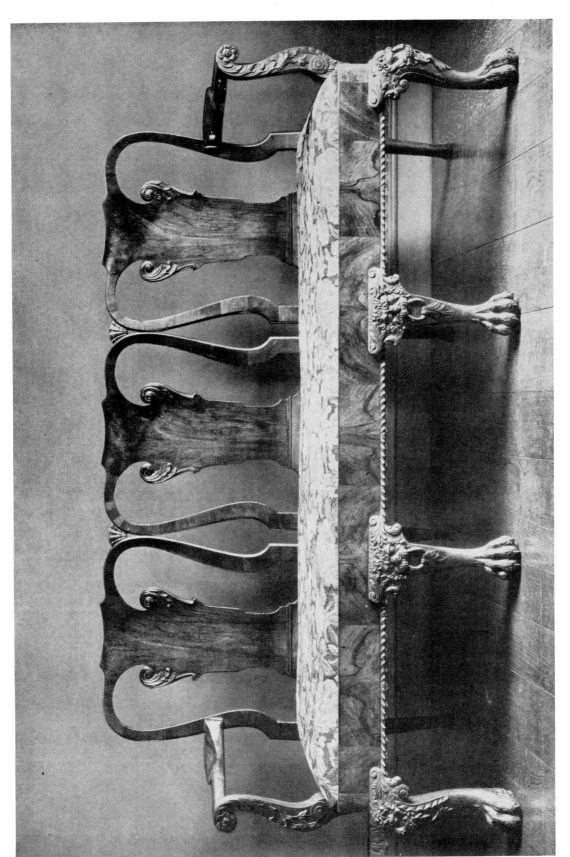

FIG. 10.—WALNUT SETTEE OF THREE-CHAIR BACKED DESIGN.   CIRCA 1730.   THIS SETTEE IS ONE OF A PAIR.

22

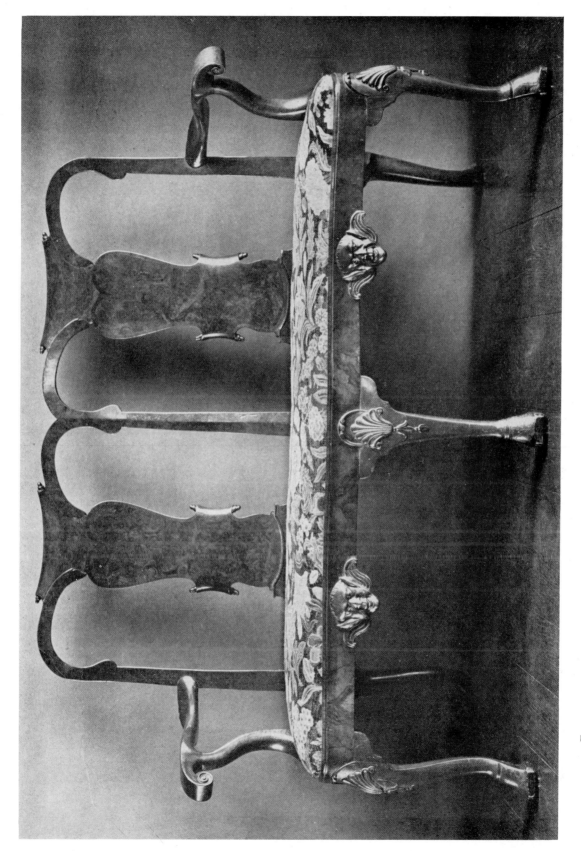

FIG. 11.—WALNUT SETTEE.   CIRCA 1720.   THE FOUNDATION TO THE SPLATS, ALSO THE BACK LEGS, ARE OF BEECH.

23

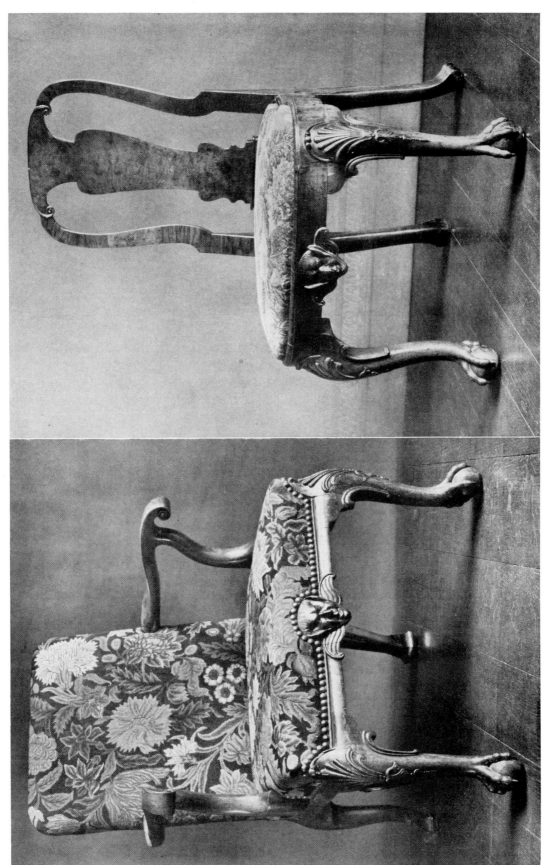

Fig. 12.—Walnut armchair with petit-point needlework covering, circa 1725. Notice the similarity of the arms and mask to those of the settee, Fig. 11.

Fig. 13.—Walnut chair with foundation to splat, and back legs, of beech. Circa 1725. The legs and the mask on the seat rail are of the same design as those of the armchair, Fig. 12.

24

Sometimes the sides of chests and the lower parts of bureau cabinets and long-case clocks are curved outwards in the form known as *bombé*, although this is more typical of Dutch furniture than English.   Indeed, this Georgian style was very strongly Dutch as regards its design in the first twenty years, after which it became anglicised and was influenced by the various phases of design which then came into vogue.   Among such phases may be included the use of the mask head *motif*.   This led to the legs and seat rails of chairs, and the legs and friezes of tables being decorated with masks—sometimes grotesque human masks (figs. 12 and 13), but more often lion masks (fig. 10).   When the lion mask *motif* decorated the knee, the foot was usually a paw foot instead of the claw and ball.   The origin of this mask *motif*, its sudden appearance and its short duration—it would appear to have come in about 1725-30 and to have lasted until about 1740-45—are difficult to account for.

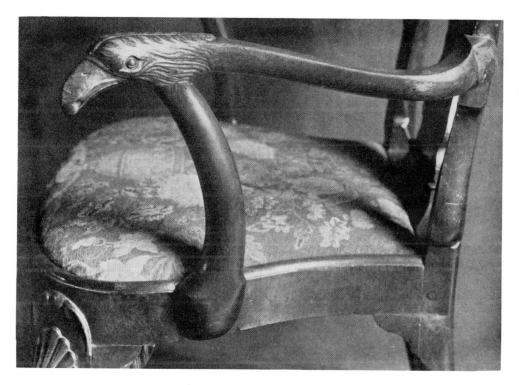

FIG. 14.—DETAIL OF ARM OF WALNUT CHAIR, ILLUSTRATED FIG. 97.

Eagle, lion, and dog heads were also *motifs* used for decorating the arms of chairs and settees (figs. 14, 16, 19 and 20).   The eagle head motif, too, is found occurring on mirrors and the legs of tables and chairs (figs. 15 and 22)*.   Another phase was the architectural treatment of the bookcase, cabinet and bureau cabinet.   Such pieces were not only based on architectural proportions, but were designed with classical pilasters and entablature surmounted by a pediment (figs. 61 and 64).   The French, Chinese and Gothic phases

---

* The above remarks also apply equally to contemporary mahogany furniture, as these *motifs* of design were used by the cabinet-makers impartially for both walnut and mahogany furniture.

of design which came into fashion about 1750-60 did not affect walnut furniture to any marked degree, since, by that time, walnut had already been relegated by mahogany to a secondary place. Such designs were carried out in the now fashionable mahogany furniture, whereas in the walnut pieces the earlier designs were still being followed. As an example of this, a walnut spinet case with engraved brass strap hinges can be quoted, which, in design, would appear to have been made in the reign of George I., and yet is dated above the keyboard 1758.

A changing feature of design which is of particular interest, in so far as it affords a somewhat rough and ready means of gauging the approximate date of a piece, may be noted in connection with the mouldings surrounding drawers. In the Stuart period of walnut furniture, the drawer was surrounded by a half-round cross-grained moulding. Unlike the drawers of the previous Cromwellian period, when the fronts were decorated with mouldings applied on them, this half-round moulding was applied on the rails between the drawers and on the edges of the sides of the piece (Diagram 1a). This moulding "ran out" at the top and bottom, as it did not go above the top drawer nor under the bottom drawer (figs. 31 and 32). In the reign of William and Mary this moulding changed in section, becoming a double cross-banded bead (Diagram 1b). In Queen Anne's reign this method of giving a decorative finish to a drawer front by ornamenting the surface

FIG. 15.—CORNER CHAIR OF CHERRY WOOD, WITH THE UNUSUAL FEATURE OF EAGLE HEADS DECORATING THE KNEE OF THE CABRIOLE LEG.   CIRCA 1745.

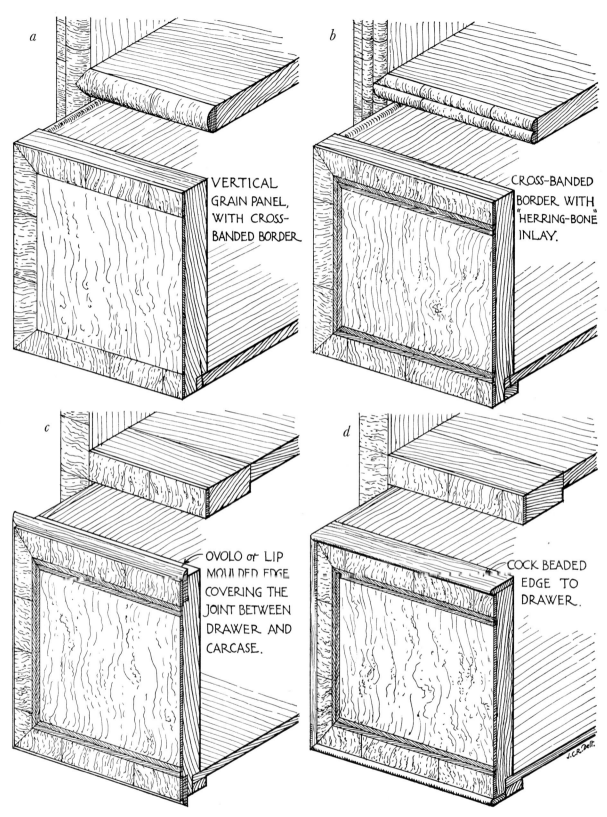

a — VERTICAL GRAIN PANEL, WITH CROSS-BANDED BORDER

b — CROSS-BANDED BORDER WITH "HERRING-BONE" INLAY.

c — OVOLO or LIP MOULDED EDGE COVERING THE JOINT BETWEEN DRAWER AND CARCASE.

d — COCK BEADED EDGE TO DRAWER.

J.C.R.Delt.

Diagram 1.—DETAILS OF MOULDINGS DECORATING DRAWERS

surrounding the drawer with a moulding was radically altered by transferring the moulding to the drawer front itself and leaving the surround plain. This was accomplished by finishing the edge of the drawer front with a lip moulding of ovolo section which hid the joint between the drawer and its opening, as it projected about ¼ inch over the surrounding surface (Diagram 1*c*). Such a method of finishing a drawer front was much in vogue on the Continent many years before its introduction into England. It persisted in English walnut furniture for about thirty to thirty-five years, as examples later than 1745 seldom possess it. About 1715, another design, known as the cock bead, was introduced for the finish to a drawer. It consisted of a half-round bead slightly projecting above the surface of the front, fixed on to the extreme edge of the drawer (Diagram 1*d*). This design is found up to the end of the eighteenth century, and was used as a finish to drawers, both in walnut and mahogany furniture. The lip moulding is also found both in walnut and mahogany furniture, as it was in vogue when these two woods were being used contemporaneously.

The above four methods of decorating the edges of drawers were

FIG. 16.—DETAIL OF ARM, SHOWING ANIMAL HEAD MOTIF OF WALNUT CHAIR, FIG. 18.

used so universally in walnut furniture during the periods mentioned that it is rare to find a piece which has a different treatment. A number of pieces are extant, however, in which the drawer fronts and their surrounds are flush, without any mouldings whatsoever (fig. 33). This flush-fronted drawer, although infrequent in English furniture, was a very common feature in French and Flemish pieces, especially those decorated with marquetry. Another variation

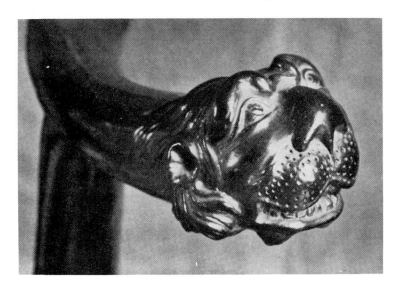

FIG. 17.—DETAIL OF ARM OF A MAHOGANY SETTEE, SHOWING ANIMAL HEAD MOTIF.

FIG. 18.—WALNUT MASTER'S CHAIR.   CIRCA 1730.   THE FOUNDATION OF THE SPLAT IS DEAL, AND THE
EAGLE AND ACANTHUS ORNAMENT ARE OF DEAL GILT.   HEIGHT 6 FEET 9 INCHES.   FOR DETAIL, SEE FIG. 16.

29

of design in the finish to drawers may be observed when the cock bead, instead of being fixed to the edge of the drawer front, is fixed on the edge of the drawer opening (Diagram 4*d*). This design is only occasionally met with, and, as pieces of furniture with this type of cock bead date from about 1720-50, it cannot be considered a transitional form between the double beaded moulding and the cock bead fixed to the drawer front.

The fact that all cabinet-makers, who were making walnut furniture throughout the country, employed the same design of drawer mouldings shows to what a remarkable extent furniture was ruled by the spirit of traditionalism in design. It took time for a new type of moulding to reach the provincial towns. There was, there-

FIG. 19.—DETAIL OF ARM, SHOWING LION HEAD MOTIF, OF WALNUT CHAIR, FIG. 95

FIG. 20.—DETAIL OF DOG'S HEAD TERMINATING ARM OF MAHOGANY CHAIR, FIG. 168

fore, considerable overlapping in the use of these various designs by the London and the provincial cabinet-maker. The latter adhered to the old designs for perhaps five or ten years after the former had been making his furniture of the current design. Cabinet-makers and joiners situated in remote country districts copied these drawer mouldings for pieces, made in the solid, of oak and such woods as elm, beech, chestnut and fruit woods, three or four decades after they had gone out of fashion in the furniture of London make. An example of this can be cited in the drawers of oak dressers and chests-with-drawers, dating as late as 1775, which were made with the overlapping lip moulding that had ceased to be used with walnut and mahogany furniture thirty years before.

MATERIAL :

ENGLISH, CONTINENTAL AND VIRGINIA WALNUT.

In considering walnut furniture from the point of view of material, it must be first of all understood that it was made from two species of the walnut tree. One was known as the European or common walnut, called *Juglans regia*, and the other, *Juglans nigra*, was the black Virginia walnut, which came from North America. The first kind was grown in England and on the Continent. Evelyn mentions the English variety of walnut when, in his *Sylva*, he writes " . . . . in the *Wall-nut*, you shall find, when 'tis *old*, that the *Wood* is admirably *figur'd*, and as it were *marbl'd*, and therefore much more esteemed by the *Joyners*, *Cabinet-makers*, &c. then the *Young*, which is *paler* of *Colour*, and without any notable *Grain*, as they call it. For the *Rain* distilling along the *Branches*, when many of them break out into clusters from the *stem*, sinks *in*, and is the *Cause* of these *marks* : since we find it exceedingly full of *pores*." He also refers to the French variety " . . . . as that which we have from *Bologno* very black of *Colour*, and so admirably streaked, as to represent natural *flowers*, *Landskips*, and other Fancys . . . ."

FIG. 21.—WALNUT CHAIR.   CIRCA 1695.   THIS TYPE OF CHAIR IS STRONGLY CONTINENTAL IN DESIGN, ALTHOUGH ITS FOREIGN COUNTERPART IS USUALLY MORE ELABORATE.   THIS CHAIR IS ONE OF A PAIR.

Evelyn praises the black Virginia walnut when he says " the *Timber* much to be preferred, and we might propagate more of them if we were careful to procure them out of *Virginia*, where they abound, or from *Grenoble*, which our *Cabinet-makers* so prize."

It would appear that from 1660-1720 English walnut was employed by the cabinet-makers, and that they sometimes used

32

FIG. 22.—WALNUT CARD TABLE WITH UNUSUAL MOTIF OF EAGLES' HEADS DECORATING THE KNEES OF THE CABRIOLE LEGS. THE CLAWS OF THE FEET ARE SCALED.

CIRCA 1735.

imported Continental walnut in the form of veneer for pieces of fine quality. From 1720 to the end of the walnut period, they used Virginia walnut, both for work in the solid and for veneer. English walnut in this period was only employed for inferior quality and country made furniture.

In support of this theory the following note from Dr. Hunter's edition of Evelyn's *Sylva*, published in 1776, can be quoted :—" Formerly the Walnut-tree," he writes, " was much propagated for its wood ; but since the importation of Mahogany and the Virginia Walnut, it has considerably decreased in reputation."

The following remarks made by Thomas Sheraton in his *Cabinet Dictionary*, published in 1803, are also interesting in so far as they bear upon this point. " Of the walnut tree," he says, " there are three species, the English walnut and the white and black Virginia. The black Virginia was much in use for cabinet work about forty or fifty years since in England, but is now quite laid aside since the introduction of mahogany. The common English walnut tree is much paler

FIG. 23.—WALNUT CHAIR WITH BACK AND SEAT RAIL OF BURR VENEER. ONE OF A PAIR.   CIRCA 1730.

than the Virginia and cannot be used for the most common purposes." The reason for the importation of this Virginia walnut was unquestionably because the English variety had become scarce. The demand had exceeded the supply, and while the younger trees were not yet suitable for the cabinet-makers' purpose, such serious inroads had been made upon the mature and full-grown specimens as to threaten their continued supply. It was, therefore, a difficult matter to obtain walnut logs of sufficient dimensions.   In addition, this English walnut was extremely wasteful in conversion, owing to the knots and defects in the wood, which forced the cabinet-maker to confine his work within the limits imposed by the quality of the timber. That Virginia walnut was imported in preference to Continental walnut—which undoubtedly would have been cheaper—can be explained by the fact that there was a great scarcity of walnut on the Continent at this period.

Fig. 24.—Walnut card table with back legs of beech, and frieze and top of burr veneer, decorated with inlaid band of amboyna.   circa 1715.

G. S. Boulger is of the same opinion when he writes, in *Wood*, that " the severe winter of 1709 killed most of the walnut trees in Central Europe, the dead trees being bought up by the Dutch, who thus secured a ' corner ' in this wood.   So scarce was it in France that its exportation was prohibited in 1720, and mahogany, imported by the Dutch and Spaniards, largely replaced it for furniture."

About 1720 there was a marked change in the design of walnut furniture.   Up to that date the legs of chairs and tables had been slender, which strongly indicates that their design had been influenced by the limitations of the material with which the cabinet-makers were working (see figs. 24, 26 and 27).

When a leg of bold design was required, they used another wood. For example, the legs of seventeenth century tables, similar to example fig. 53, are more often found of elm than of walnut. Another expedient—when it was desired to make the cabriole leg of a Queen Anne chair at all bold in design—was to build up the timber out of which

FIG. 25.—WALNUT CARD TABLE WITH FRIEZE AND TOP OF BURR VENEER.   CIRCA 1730.
FOR DETAILS, SEE FIGS. 139 AND 217.

the leg was to be cut by gluing on pieces to obtain the necessary width of wood, which the curve of the leg required.

On the other hand, about 1720 the legs of chairs, stools and tables became bolder and stouter (see figs. 23 and 25). The cabriole was more accentuated, and the *motif* of the claw and ball foot and of the paw foot (fig. 34) was used to terminate the leg. Such a leg required a much more substantial block of timber for its execution than had been hitherto obtainable, yet the majority of examples of this description are found carved out of one piece of wood and not built up.

One possible explanation for the boldness of the design of the chair and table legs and the chair arms which came into vogue about 1720 is that the cabinet-makers had access to a supply of material which could be obtained in greater bulk than they had hitherto used. The evidence from Dr. Hunter's and Sheraton's quotations is definite proof that the cabinet-makers did use Virginia walnut, and therefore it is not too much to presume that the furniture of this bold design, dating from 1720 to the end of the walnut period, was made of Virginia walnut, and that the earlier furniture of the more circumspect and restricted type was made of English walnut. On the face of this evidence it would also appear that the cabinet-makers began to use the former wood about 1720, which coincides with the time when they altered the design of their furniture. This is a very definite example of design being governed by material.

Virginia walnut would appear to have been used both for work in the solid and also in the form of veneer ; this latter, however, only for furniture of good quality, as it would appear from the following quotation from Dr. Hunter's edition of Evelyn's *Sylva* that this variety of walnut was highly prized when the wood was finely figured.

FIG. 26.—SMALL WALNUT HALF-CIRCULAR TABLE.   CIRCA 1720.

" The black Virginia Walnut," he writes, " is much more inclinable to grow upright than the common sort, and the wood being generally of a more beautiful grain, renders

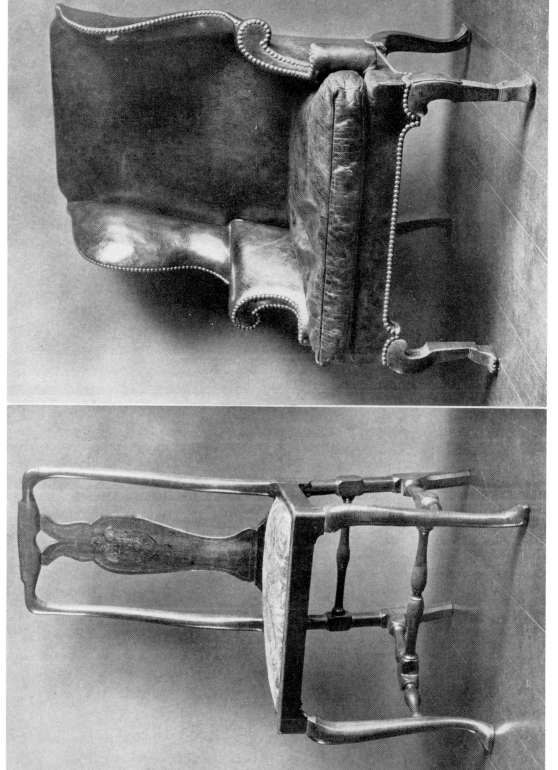

FIG. 27.—WALNUT CHAIR WITH SPLAT DECORATED WITH MARQUETRY
PANEL.   CIRCA 1710.   THIS CHAIR IS ONE OF A PAIR

FIG. 28.—WINGED ARMCHAIR WITH WALNUT LEGS DECORATED WITH ARABESQUE
MARQUETRY PANELS.   CIRCA 1720.

37

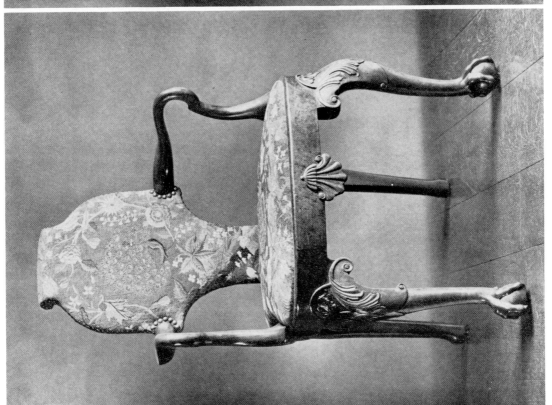

FIG. 29.—WALNUT ARMCHAIR WITH PETIT-POINT NEEDLEWORK COVERING. CIRCA 1730. NOTICE THE SIMILARITY TO THE STOOL, FIG. 82, AS REGARDS THE USE OF THE INVERTED SHELL MOTIF ON THE SEAT RAIL.

FIG. 30.—WALNUT ARMCHAIR OF UNUSUAL DESIGN WITH CROSS STRETCHERS AND ORIGINAL PETIT-POINT NEEDLEWORK COVERING. CIRCA 1710. THIS CHAIR IS ONE OF A PAIR.

38

it preferable to that, and better worth cultivating.   I have seen some of this wood beautifully veined with black and white, which, when polished, has appeared at a distance like veined marble.   This wood is greatly esteemed by the cabinet-makers for inlaying, as also for bedsteads, chairs, tables and cabinets ; and is one of the most durable woods for those purposes of English growth, being less liable to be infected with insects than most other kinds (which may proceed from its extraordinary bitterness) ; but it is not proper for buildings of strength, it being of a brittle nature, and exceedingly subject to break very short, though it commonly gives notice by its crackling some time before it breaks."

The wood, however, when used in the solid, does not exhibit to the same degree the black markings of the English and Continental walnut.   It is a harder and smoother wood than these varieties and the grain is straight and even, although sometimes, as already mentioned, it had a beautiful figure.   The colour is a darker tone than the English walnut, and, when in its unpolished state, such as when used for drawer linings, it is almost a plum colour.   From pieces extant made of Virginia walnut it can be seen sometimes that the dark tone has bleached through exposure to the light to a pale grey brown.

Even in the period when Virginia walnut was employed by the cabinet-makers, economy was an object.   For instance, indigenous and therefore cheaper woods than Virginia walnut, such as beech and elm, were used for the foundations of the veneered splats and the back legs of chairs and settees.   Since the back legs and side rails were made out of one piece, which required a log of large dimensions, a great saving was assured by the use of these commoner woods (figs. 11 and 13).

In the seventeenth century Continental walnut would appear to have been imported. Proof of this is to be found in the two quotations already cited from Evelyn, where he mentions walnut from Boulogne and Grenoble, the former being " admirably streaked," and the latter " which our cabinet-makers so prize."   As, in the first case, Evelyn praises the figure of the wood, it was undoubtedly used in the form of veneer, and most probably the latter was also so employed.

Evelyn bears testimony to the use of beech, owing to the scarcity of walnut in the seventeenth century, when he writes : " . . . . . were this Timber in greater plenty amongst us, we should have far better *Utensils* of all sorts for our Houses, as *Chairs, Stools, Bedsteads, Tables, Wainscot, Cabinets*, etc, instead of the more vulgar *Beech*, subject to the *worm,* weak, and unsightly ; but which to counterfeit and deceive the unwary, they wash over with a *decoction* made of the *Green husks* of *Walnuts*, etc, I say, had we store of this *material,* we should find an incredible improvement in the more stable *Furniture* of our Houses . . . ."

Many seventeenth century chairs and stools have survived made of beech, chestnut* and elm, which goes to prove the truth of Evelyn's statement.

---

* Dr. Hunter writes about chestnut : " Of the Chestnut are made very fine tables, stools, chairs, chests and bedsteads." See also Chair illustrated (Fig. 89).

VENEERED WALNUT FURNITURE.

That Evelyn as early as 1664, the date of the publication of the first edition of his *Sylva*, should deplore the fact that furniture of beech wood was being made to imitate walnut is especially illuminating, since it shows how the vogue for the new walnut furniture had ousted the old-fashioned oak pieces, so much so, indeed, that people preferred their furniture made of even an inferior wood, which resembled walnut, rather than of the unfashionable oak. Writing in the second edition of *Sylva*, published in 1670, Evelyn declares that " . . . . our late *Pride, Effeminacy* and *Luxurie* (which has to our vast *charges* excluded all the *Ornaments* of *Timber, etc.* to give place to *Hangings, Embroideries* and forrain *Leather*) shall be put out of Countenance, we may hope to see a *new face* of things, for the encouragement of *Planters*, the more immediate Work of *Gods* hands ; and the natural, wholesome, and ancient *use* of *Timber*, for the more *lasting occasions* and *furniture* of our *Dwellings :* And though I do not speak all this for the sake of *Joyne-stools, Benches, Cup-boards, Massy Tables* and Gygantic Bed-steds, the hospitable *Utensils* of our fore-*Fathers ;* Yet I would be glad to encourage the *Carpenter* and the *Joyner*, and rejoyce to see, that their *Work* and *Skil* do dayly improve ; "

These remarks certainly give an insight into the revolutionary changes which took place in furniture in the first ten years of Charles II.'s reign. Chairs and stools were now made of walnut instead of oak ; the seats, instead of being of solid wood, were of cane, the backs likewise were fitted with cane panels in order to make them more yielding and comfortable than were the oak panelled backs of the pre-Restoration period. Tables, chests-with-drawers, cabinets and other articles of domestic furniture were also made of walnut, but, in these pieces, the surfaces were of veneered walnut and not of solid wood, as was the case with the chairs. Up to the present time it has been considered by various authorities that chairs, stools and day-beds made in the solid walnut, date from the beginning of Charles II.'s reign, and earlier, but that veneered and marquetry furniture was not made previous to 1675. In the first edition of Evelyn's *Sylva*, published in 1664, there is abundant evidence, beyond and apart from that already quoted, to confute this erroneous statement. He writes : " It [walnut] is of singular account with . . . . the *Cabinet-maker* for *Inlayings*, especially the firm and close *Timber* about the *Roots*, which is admirable for *fleck'd* and *chambletted* works, and the older it is, the more estimable." He also says as regards maple that "The *Timber* is far superiour to *Beech* for all uses of the *Turner*, ... as the *Joyner* for *Tables, Inlayings*, and for the delicateness of the grain when the *knurs* and *nodosities* are rarely *diapred*, which does much advance its price : " Then again, when discussing box : " . . . . the Roots of this Tree do furnish the *Inlayer* and *Cabinet-makers* with pieces rarely *undulated*, and full of variety." Pepys also brings contemporary evidence to bear on this point when he mentions in his diary that, on March 25th, 1667, he found his friend Mr. Povey, " at work with a cabinet-maker making of a new inlaid table."

In the second edition of *Sylva*, published in 1670, Evelyn definitely mentions marquetry and also veneering. After giving a list of various coloured woods used by " our inlayers," he goes on to say : " . . . . but when they would imitate the naturall turning of *Leaves*

Fig. 31.—Chest-with-drawers on stand.   circa 1690.   The panels are of burr ash veneer, the surrounds to the panels are of straight-grained walnut, the herring-bone banding is of ash, and the cross-grained mouldings and turned legs are of yew.   The combination of so many woods, the fine proportions and the good design of this piece make it of exceptional interest.

FIG. 32.—WALNUT CHEST-WITH DRAWERS ON STAND.   CIRCA 1710.
AN UNUSUAL FEATURE OF THIS PIECE IS THAT THE SIDES ARE OF SOLID WALNUT AND NOT VENEERED.

in their curious *Compartiments* and bordures of *Flower-works*, they effect it by dipping the pieces (first cut into shape and ready to *In-lay*) so far into *hot Sand*, as they would have the Shadow, and the heat of the *Sand* darkens it so gradually, without detriment or burning the thin Chip, as one would conceive it to be natural : *Note*, that the *Sand* is to be heated in some very thin Brasse pan like to the bottom of a Scale or *Ballance* : This I mention because the burning with *Irons*, or *Aqua-fortis*, is not comparable to it."

Evelyn mentions veneering when he is discussing cedar wood. "It might be done with moderate Expense," he writes, "especially, in some small proportions, and in *Faneering*, as they term it, and mouldings . . . ."*

Apart from the last two quotations, which are definite proof that walnut veneered and marquetry furniture was made in England in 1670, the earlier quotations of 1664, referring to "inlayings" or "inlayer," must also refer to veneered furniture. It is unlikely that the earlier mention of "inlayings" applied to the method of inlaying thin pieces of coloured wood to form a pattern into a solid background which was cut out to receive them, especially in view of the fact that no examples of such solid inlaid walnut furniture have survived of this period. Inlaid work of this type, a favourite method of decoration to oak pieces in the Elizabethan and early Jacobean periods, had gone out of fashion by the middle of the seventeenth century.

It has been thought necessary to go to some length to show that veneered walnut and marquetry furniture was being made in England as early as 1664, as in the most recent books on furniture, illustrating veneered walnut, marquetry and parquetry pieces of the first half of Charles II.'s reign, such pieces have all been dated not earlier than 1675, and in some instances as late as 1700.

An event which must have created a considerable demand for new furniture was the devastating Fire of London in the year 1666. It is only natural to infer that this immediate and sudden call for furniture must have been met by London cabinet-makers with pieces in the latest fashion, which would unquestionably be of walnut veneer. Furniture in the solid of oak and soft woods, such as beech, must also have been made in considerable quantities to supply the needs of the poorer classes.

One reason advanced at the present time to support the theory that cabinet-makers were not making veneered furniture in the early years of Charles II.'s reign is that there are no transitional pieces, and that both veneered and marquetry furniture appeared in England in a fully developed state. Its sudden appearance is put down to the fact that all of it was made by alien craftsmen; whereas, on the contrary, there are pieces of veneered walnut furniture extant which are definitely transitional. Such pieces generally take the form of chests-with-drawers, the earliest transitional examples of which date from the Cromwellian period. The fronts of the drawers are decorated with applied mouldings, a typical feature of Jacobean furniture, and the drawer fronts within the mouldings are covered with walnut veneer ⅛ of an inch or more in thickness. In fact, sometimes so thick is this veneer that it is more in the nature of a thin slab. The mouldings are of straight run walnut, and the sides of the chest are panelled in oak. The workmanship

---

* Presumably, the mention of the word "mouldings" applies here to cross-grained mouldings.

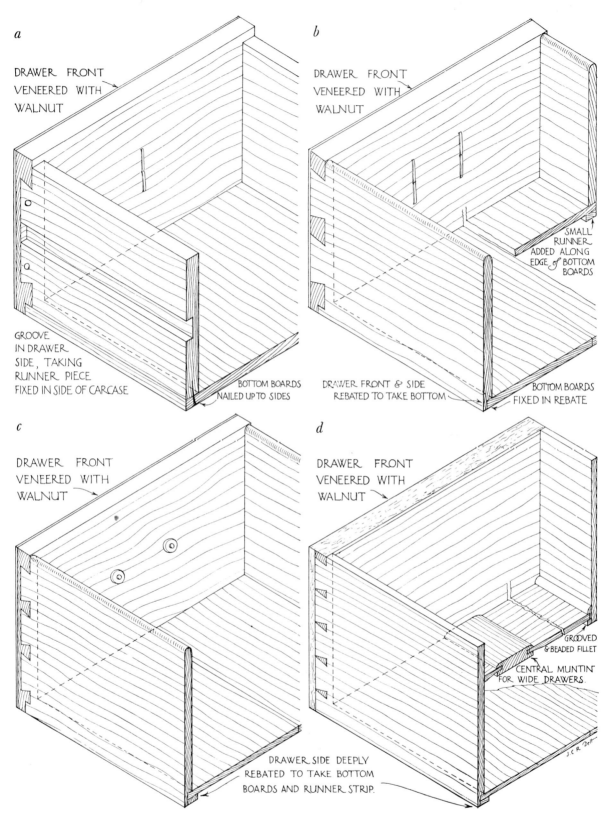

a

DRAWER FRONT
VENEERED WITH
WALNUT

GROOVE
IN DRAWER
SIDE, TAKING
RUNNER PIECE
FIXED IN SIDE OF CARCASE

BOTTOM BOARDS
NAILED UP TO SIDES

b

DRAWER FRONT
VENEERED WITH
WALNUT

SMALL
RUNNER
ADDED ALONG
EDGE of BOTTOM
BOARDS

DRAWER FRONT & SIDE
REBATED TO TAKE BOTTOM

BOTTOM BOARDS
FIXED IN REBATE

c

DRAWER FRONT
VENEERED WITH
WALNUT

DRAWER SIDE DEEPLY
REBATED TO TAKE BOTTOM
BOARDS AND RUNNER STRIP.

d

DRAWER FRONT
VENEERED WITH
WALNUT

GROOVED
& BEADED FILLET

CENTRAL MUNTIN
FOR WIDE DRAWERS.

J C R Dell

Diagram 2.—DETAILS SHOWING CONSTRUCTION OF DOVETAILS AND METHODS OF FIXING DRAWER BOTTOMS.

44

is coarse and, in construction, it is similar to the Jacobean furniture, the drawers being hung on runners (Diagram 2a). The next type of transitional chest extant must, according to sequence, be dated about 1660-5. In this form of chest, the fronts of the drawers are veneered with walnut and sometimes with parquetry ; half-round cross-grained mouldings are fixed around the drawer openings, similar to Diagram 1a. The top of the chest is veneered, and the sides are of oak, panelled in the manner of Jacobean furniture.

There is no question but that the English cabinet-maker learnt how to cut veneer and the method of laying it down from Continental practice, and the fact that there were alien craftsmen in this country who, by their teaching, assisted the English to learn the art of veneering and marquetry cutting, is not disputed. But the survival of transitional pieces, and the gradual improvement in the quality of workmanship, both as regards walnut and marquetry furniture—which latter will be discussed later—is very strong evidence in support of the assertion that the majority of the veneered walnut, parquetry and marquetry furniture was made by English craftsmen. It is true there were skilled foreign cabinet-makers domiciled in England who undoubtedly followed their craft by making similar pieces to those of the English ; but the productions of these men would not have shown any transitional phases as regards craftsmanship, as was the case with the English work. They were skilled in veneering and marquetry, as the French, Flemings and the Dutch had made this type of furniture long before it had begun to be produced in England. The work of such aliens would be, therefore, of a far higher standard than that produced by the English craftsmen. This especially applies to marquetry work. Later in the chapter this question of the work of alien craftsmen will be dealt with more fully.

In the veneered walnut furniture made by the English craftsmen there is a definite sequence, displaying a gradual evolution of refinement in workmanship, starting in the decade previous to the reign of Charles II. and continuing up to the end of the seventeenth century If this sequence had not begun until 1675, the period would have been too short for the full evolution of design, workmanship and construction to have come about.

Yet another point advanced by those who deny that veneered walnut furniture was made before 1675, is that pieces which display early methods of construction and coarseness in their execution, and exhibit a style of design peculiar to the reign of Charles II., were produced by the country cabinet-maker two or three decades after the cabinet-makers of London and the important provincial towns had ceased to make furniture of this early character.

That this line of argument is unsound becomes apparent when one considers the position of the country cabinet-maker and joiner in the walnut period. Firstly, it is extremely unlikely that he would have made walnut veneered furniture at all prior to 1700. The country cabinet-maker was engaged in supplying the requirements of people in the immediate neighbourhood, such as the yeoman farmer and the poorer country gentry, and was making cheap and common furniture for the labouring classes. It is highly improbable that the nobility would patronise the local country cabinet-maker for furniture for the salon and best rooms of their country mansions. This they would undoubtedly procure from the nearest provincial town or from London. In the last half of the walnut period, the country cabinet-maker might have made pieces of veneered walnut furniture, and such pieces, in their design and manner of construction, would most probably appear to be two or three decades earlier in date. The difference, however, between such pieces and those of the earlier period lies in the quality of the woods used in the carcase and the drawer linings. In the veneered walnut, marquetry and parquetry furniture of the Stuart period, as will be shown later, the deal of the carcase was of the finest quality, and so was the quarter-cut oak of the drawer linings, both these timbers being undoubtedly imported from abroad.

Country-made furniture can always be recognised by the inferior quality of the wood used for the drawer linings and backboards. The country cabinet-maker could not afford to use imported woods, and therefore relied upon local timber—oak, elm, beech, ash and chestnut—which, in the majority of country districts, would be cheaper than deal, as deal was not indigenous to England in this period. One year, the country cabinet-maker might have a surplus of walnut, owing to a storm having blown down a number of walnut trees in the locality. In this case he could afford to use it extravagantly by making pieces in the solid walnut. A number of country-made walnut chests-with-drawers have survived made of the solid wood. Indeed, knowledge of woods will soon dispel the notion that furniture made in the early part of the reign of Charles II. was fashioned by the country joiner in the reign of George I.

The cabinet-makers of the Stuart period of walnut furniture were not long in realising the decorative effect which could be given to a piece by the figure and grain of the wood, then made possible by the new process of veneering. They found that veneer which was cut from the root of a tree, or from where there was any irregular growth or deformity, exhibited a far more decorative marking than when the veneer was cut from the trunk, when it would usually exhibit a straight figuring, and not a " mottled " or " marbl'd " one, as Evelyn so aptly describes it. Walnut trees which had finely figured wood with curls produced by the dividing of the heart wood where a large branch joined the trunk, were far more costly for the cabinet-maker to buy than the trees which had plain and unfigured wood. The latter would be used for work in the solid, as, for example, chairs and table legs.

The front of a good quality piece would be veneered with finely figured wood—usually with what is termed burr veneer, which has a mottled figuring because, as explained above, it is cut from the root of the tree (fig. 33). For the sides of the piece, which were less noticeable, an unfigured and plain veneer would be employed. In lower quality examples, a straight-grained and plainer marked veneer would be used on the front, as this would effect a considerable saving in cost as compared with the burr veneer.

Walnut veneer was cut by hand saws, and this work was carried out by the cabinet-makers. It is also said to have been done by special workmen who, visiting the cabinet-makers' workshops once or twice a year, transformed into veneers the wood which had been specially reserved for this purpose. The old walnut veneer is found in thicknesses varying from $\frac{1}{16}$ of an inch to $\frac{1}{8}$ of an inch.

FIG. 33.—NARROW WALNUT BUREAU BOOKCASE WITH FRONT OF BURR VENEER.
CIRCA 1730.   THE TOP DRAWER IS FITTED WITH TOILET BOXES.

FIG. 34.—WALNUT CARD TABLE. CIRCA 1740. THIS IS A VERY RARE AND UNUSUAL EXAMPLE, AS NOT ONLY ARE THE FOUR LEGS DECORATED WITH LION MASKS, BUT THE FRONT OF THE TABLE IS OF SERPENTINE SHAPE. FOR DETAIL, SEE FIG. 72.

48

Fig. 35.—Walnut bureau bookcase with double-domed top.   c. 1715

Fig. 36.—Framed saw for cutting timber, driven by water.
from an engraving in Evelyn's "sylva," 1670.

A framed saw worked by water power for sawing timber is shown in fig. 36. This illustration is from an engraving in the second edition of Evelyn's *Sylva*. In describing these machines, Evelyn says : " . . . . the *Norway Engine*, or *Saw-Mill*, to be either *moved* with the force of *Water*, or *Wind*, &c, for the more expedite *cuting* and converting of *Timber*, to which we will add another, for the more facile *perforation* and boring of *Elms*, or other *Timber* to make *Pipes* and *Aquaeducts* . . . ."

In a good quality piece, considerable care and skill was required in the symmetrical setting out of the figure of the veneer on a drawer front or cabinet door. Pieces of veneer cut in successive layers from the same log exhibited the same figuring, and therefore such pieces, when laid together so that the markings joined, made a symmetrical pattern. The veneer on the top of a table would consist of four pieces with similar figuring in each. Each piece formed a quarter of the top, which resulted in the figuring being of a symmetrical form. The setting of the veneer in this manner was called quartering.

FIG. 37.—WALNUT DRESSING TABLE WITH DRAWER FITTED WITH TOILET BOXES AND COMPARTMENTS   CIRCA 1745.
THE WALNUT TOILET MIRROR DATES ABOUT 1730.

Drawer fronts would be veneered with two or four pieces of the same figured wood, so that one half of the drawer front would resemble the other, the grain running across the width of the front (fig. 37). In poor quality pieces the cabinet-maker did not go to the same trouble to match his veneers in this manner, and, in consequence, the decorative value of the piece was diminished.

Furniture, besides being decorated with the burr and the straight-grained veneer of walnut, was also veneered with the burr wood of elm, ash (fig. 31), maple, yew, oak, cherry and plum, as the cabinet-makers had discovered that the veneer cut from the roots of these trees had an extremely decorative effect.*   Examples extant in these woods are, however, far fewer than are those of walnut ; while after the reign of Queen Anne, the vogue for the use of such woods would appear to have declined, with perhaps the possible exception of burr elm and yew, as a number of pieces veneered with these woods have survived, dating as late as 1760.   Late pieces veneered with elm often exhibit a coarseness of workmanship, and the wood of the carcasing and drawer linings is of the poorest quality.   It would appear, therefore, that elm was used sometimes in the form of veneer by the country cabinet-maker, owing to the scarcity of walnut, in his immediate locality.

It was in the first half of the walnut period that the cabinet-makers made the fullest use of finely figured woods, employed in the form of veneers, for the decoration of furniture. Marquetry and parquetry were other methods of decoration much used during this period.

MARQUETRY FURNITURE.

There were two distinct varieties of marquetry belonging to the Stuart period of 1660-90, although both had the marquetry contained in panels.   The first was of a design composed of arabesque acanthus leaf scrolls, generally with flowers introduced, and also birds, usually of the eagle species, although parrots were sometimes employed as an alternative.   This type of marquetry generally had the acanthus scrolls in walnut and the flowers in a red coloured wood on a light background, generally of holly (fig. 38). The early examples, which date from the first decade of Charles II.'s reign, display a distinct coarseness in the cutting of the marquetry, whereas the later examples show much finer workmanship.   In these, a dark wood is often employed in the pattern, and sometimes the background is of walnut instead of holly (fig. 39).   In such pieces the eagle occurs more frequently than in the earlier ones.   The surrounds to the marquetry panels were usually filled with straight cut veneer (figs. 38, 39).   This type of acanthus scroll marquetry was copied by the English from Continental work.   Seventeenth century pieces of South German *provenance* are extant, decorated with marquetry panels of a very similar character.   The eagle *motif* was also a very favourite one with Continental designers.

The second variety of marquetry was entirely different, as it was composed of a design of naturalistic flowers arranged in groups and sometimes in vases without any arabesque scrolls.   Of this floral marquetry there appear to have been two distinct schools.   The first and, perhaps, earliest school, like the acanthus scroll marquetry, shows from extant examples that the early pieces dating from 1660-75 have a crudeness and stiffness in the design and a coarseness in the execution.   The flowers are sparsely placed and do not intertwine with each other as in the later examples which exhibit the finest work (fig. 40). Up to about 1690, this type of marquetry was designed in panels, the surrounds to the panels being sometimes filled with walnut veneer and sometimes with oyster shell parquetry, of either walnut, laburnum or olive wood.   This oyster shell veneer was obtained by

* Amboyna, Thuya and Kingwood were other woods used on account of their fine figure.

FIG. 38.—(ABOVE) TOP OF CHEST-WITH-DRAWERS DECORATED WITH MARQUETRY, WITH BACKGROUND OF HOLLY AND PATTERN OF WALNUT AND COLOURED WOODS. CIRCA 1670.

FIG. 39.—(BELOW) TOP OF CHEST-WITH-DRAWERS DECORATED WITH MARQUETRY, WITH BACKGROUND OF WALNUT CIRCA 1670.

F 53

FIG. 40.—MIRROR WITH FRAME DECORATED WITH FLORAL MARQUETRY. C. 1680. THE FOLIAGE IS STAINED GREEN.

FIG. 41.—CABINET DOOR DECORATED WITH FLORAL MARQUETRY OF COLOURED WOODS.   THE JASMINE FLOWERS
ARE OF IVORY, AND MANY OF THE LEAVES ARE ALSO IVORY, BUT STAINED GREEN.   CIRCA 1675.

Fig. 42.—Detail of door of small long-case clock, Fig. 48.

Fig. 43.—DETAIL OF DOOR OF CLOCK CASE, SHOWING FLORAL MARQUETRY OF THE FINEST QUALITY.   CIRCA 1690.

Fig. 44.—DETAIL OF CLOCK CASE DECORATED WITH ARABESQUE MARQUETRY.   THE BACKGROUND OF
THE DESIGN IS OF HOLLYWOOD.   NOTE HOW THE HOLLYWOOD VENEER IS PIECED TOGETHER BY A
WAVED LINE BETWEEN THE PATTERN AND THE CROSS-GRAINED MOULDING.   CIRCA 1695.

58

sawing the smaller branches of the tree transversely at an oblique angle. The veneer obtained in this manner produced an oval figure similar to the shell of an oyster. The flowers used in the design were the tulip, the rose, the carnation, and the jessamine. Birds were also introduced. Unlike the acanthus scroll marquetry, the background was invariably of a dark wood, usually walnut, which was sometimes stained black. In some examples the leaves of the foliage were stained green, in order to give a more realistic appearance.

In a *Treatise of Japanning and Varnishing*, by John Stalker, published in 1688, there is given a recipe of how " To Dye or Stain Woods of any colour, for Inlaid or Flower'd work, done by the Cabinet-makers." In his description of the process of staining, John Stalker mentions " reds, blews, greens, or what colour best please you." He also shows how the woods can be stained different shades of the same colour, a process which, he says, " . . . . contributes much to the beauty and neatness of the work, and agrees with the nature of your parti-coloured flowers." From this it would appear that this floral marquetry had other artificial colours introduced into its design besides green, although no genuine example has been recorded with blue flowers. Examples with a dark red wood have survived, however, which, in some cases, may have been pear wood stained red, as Stalker describes in his recipe. The non-survival of the blue stain may be due, either to it having faded, or else to the uncommonness of such treatment. This old recipe is interesting in so far as it shows that the original idea of this floral marquetry was to make it appear as realistic as possible.

The second school of floral marquetry resembles much more closely the contemporary Flemish marquetry ; in fact, in some cases they are so much alike that it would be impossible to tell one from the other, were it not for the contributory evidence of the construction, the woods of the carcase and the locks to the drawers.

In comparing the examples extant of both schools, it will be found that the marquetry of the second has a more brilliant and contrasting effect, which is due to the background invariably being of a dark tone, sometimes of ebony. Ivory constantly occurs in the design, either in the form of leaves when it is dyed green, or for the petals of the jessamine flowers when it is left in its natural state. The difference between the two varieties, the sober and subdued tone of the one and the brilliant pictorial effect of the other, can be gathered from examples illustrated (figs. 41 and 42). In the English-Flemish marquetry, birds and butterflies more frequently appear in the design, while the inside of cabinet doors and the sides of cabinets are often inlaid with parrots in oval medallions.

Judging from extant pieces, this marquetry was always designed in panels, the surrounds of which were of oyster-shell veneer, usually of olive or laburnum wood, and not from the straight-grained walnut, which is more typical of the first school.

It is extremely difficult to find a reason for the existence of these two schools of floral marquetry, flourishing side by side. The second school also had its early pieces, which like the first school show a lack of spontaneity in design and a coarseness in the workmanship (fig. 45). One other curious unexplained fact is that, although pieces such as chests-with-drawers, tables, cabinets, and mirror frames will be found decorated with both types of floral marquetry, only a few examples of the longcase clock have survived of the English-Flemish variety. This is specially remarkable as the longcase clock was by far the most favourite piece for marquetry decoration, and a very large number are extant decorated with the English floral variety.

About 1690, floral marquetry of the English school was no longer confined to panels. It was now designed to cover the whole surface of a clock door or drawer front. *Amorini* and acanthus leaf arabesques in the French style were introduced into this work, which was the last and final phase of floral marquetry (fig. 43).

FIG. 45.—FALL OF WRITING CABINET DECORATED WITH FLORAL MARQUETRY; THE LEAVES ARE OF IVORY STAINED GREEN.   CIRCA 1665.

Another type of marquetry design that came into vogue in the reign of William and Mary was that known as the arabesque (fig. 44). This type with its strap work and acanthus leaf scrolls, sometimes with birds, figures and shells introduced into the pattern, was undoubtedly inspired by the contemporary designs of the famous French *ébéniste*, André Boulle. Arabesque marquetry was contrived both in panels and of the "all over" design. Sometimes the pattern was of walnut with a light background of holly; while other examples will display the reverse: a dark background and a light design.

FIG. 46.—FALL OF BUREAU DECORATED WITH SEAWEED MARQUETRY IN PANELS ; THE SURROUNDS TO THE PANELS ARE OF PARQUETRY OF KINGWOOD.   CIRCA 1695.

Another variety of marquetry, known as the seaweed or endive, was also in vogue in the reign of William and Mary (fig. 46). The appellation of "endive" was given to it because it resembled the plant of this name. Seaweed marquetry in its pure form had no arabesque strapwork, figures or birds. Early examples of it are found about 1680, which exhibit a coarseness in the tendrils and none of the delicacy of the later work, which is so fine that it resembles lace. This marquetry was usually designed in panels and, like the arabesque, is found with a light pattern on a dark background, or *vice versa*. German and Dutch pieces are extant with marquetry very similar in character to the early examples of the English seaweed, again showing that the English craftsman copied the design in the first instance, but, having done so, at once improved and stamped it with his own special characteristics.

One other, but rarer, variety of marquetry in vogue in the reigns of William and Mary and Queen Anne was that which has been termed Persian marquetry. In this type the design was composed of eastern *motifs*, such as the crescent, horseshoe-shaped medallions, and the two-handled vase amidst conventional foliage and flowers. The design of this marquetry was inspired by Turkish and Persian embroideries. Examples of it are seldom found on anything except clock cases.

Judging from the very large number of clock cases decorated with marquetry that have survived, it would appear that marquetry was much more favoured by the case-maker of long-case clocks than by the cabinet-maker. The different varieties of marquetry continued to be used by the case-maker for a number of years after they had gone out of fashion with the cabinet-maker. Floral marquetry is found on clocks belonging to the reign of Queen Anne, and arabesque marquetry on clocks as late as 1720. The only late use of marquetry in furniture is found in the decoration of splats and legs of chairs (figs. 47 and 28), and in exceptional examples of the bureau bookcase which occasionally have small panels of the arabesque type. Such decoration was fashionable in furniture up till the end of the reign of George I.

It has already been mentioned in connection with walnut veneered furniture of the Stuart period, that, as it showed a distinct evolution with regard to quality of workmanship, the majority of it must have been made by English craftsmen, and that exceptional pieces only can be placed to the credit of alien craftsmen.   As, therefore, there is also a distinct evolution in the quality of marquetry work, the same conclusion should be justifiable with regard to it.   An alien craftsman working in England, early in the reign of Charles II., would not have been guilty of making marquetry of poor quality, since he would be an experienced and qualified craftsman, as marquetry, on the Continent, had long passed the initial stages of an undeveloped craft.

FIG. 47.—DETAIL OF BACK OF WALNUT CHAIR ILLUSTRATED
IN FIG. 90.

This applies equally to France, Flanders, and Holland. It is, therefore, permissible to assume that the early pieces of the Charles II. period that show a somewhat primitive rendering of the design and a coarseness in quality, similar to fig. 45, were made by English craftsmen, and that work of superlative quality, similar to fig. 41, was made by alien craftsmen.

In the seventeenth century, there were Huguenot and Dutch craftsmen working here as cabinet-makers, and these men held important positions in the trade, as, for example, Gerreit Jensen, the Dutchman, of whom there is a record that he supplied Charles II. with inlaid furniture. He also made furniture for the Royal palaces in the reign of William III. It is to such alien craftsmen that veneered walnut and marquetry furniture of superlative quality is due. In the design of this furniture a foreign feeling is noticeable. This especially applies to clock cases, of which some very fine marquetry specimens are extant (see detail of door, fig. 43), which have features such as panels on the sides, with arched tops formed by cross-banded edgings, and a four-sided dome to the hood (instead of three-sided as in the English clocks), which denote Continental and not English practice.   Spiral twist turning on pieces made by alien craftsmen has the Continental single rope twist, and not the English " barley sugar " (Diagram 3).   Legs to tables and cabinet stands, and the columns to the hoods of long-case clocks, are cases in point.   Unless such pieces, however, also exhibit English characteristics as regards the carcase woods, drawer linings, dovetails, and locks, they must be considered of foreign *provenance* and not the work of the alien craftsman settled in England.

This superior quality veneered walnut and marquetry furniture is outside the evolution of the furniture made by English craftsmen from 1660-1700. Eliminate this type and a

definite evolution of refinement in quality of workmanship can be traced in the furniture of this period. Contemporary evidence, which goes to prove this, has been handed down to us by John Evelyn, who, in *An Account of Architects and Architecture*, published in 1696-97, says of English craftsmen :—" For we daily find that when once they arrive to a thorough Inspection and Address in their *Trades*, they Paragon, if not Exceed even the most Exquisite of other Countries, as we may see in that late Reformation and Improvement of our *Lock-smiths* work, *Joyners*, *Cabinet-makers* and the like, who from very Vulgar and Pitiful *Artists*, are now come to Produce *Works* as Curious for the *Filing*, and admirable for their Dexterity in *Contriving*, as any we meet with abroad, ..."

In the reign of Queen Anne, these alien craftsmen had settled down in England and had become anglicised : for example, Jensen changed his name to Gerard Johnson. There must have been many other alien craftsmen who came to this country and did likewise, but, unfortunately, their names have been lost to us, as they did not have the patronage of the sovereign as had Jensen, whose name in consequence has been preserved in the Royal accounts.

The illustration (fig. 42) shows the detail of the marquetry in the door of the small long-case clock (fig. 48). If this is compared with the detail of the marquetry panel (fig. 43), it will be seen to be

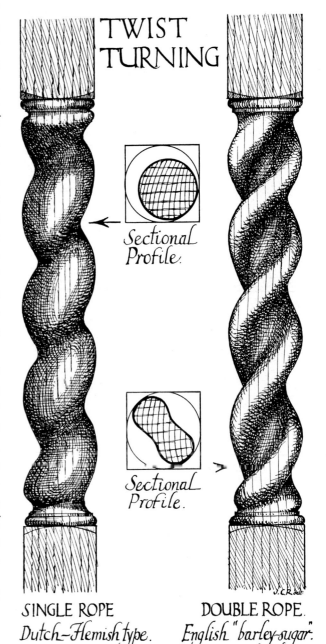

TWIST TURNING

Sectional Profile.

Sectional Profile.

SINGLE ROPE
Dutch-Flemish type.

DOUBLE ROPE.
English "barley-sugar".

Diagram 3.—DETAILS SHOWING DIFFERENCE BETWEEN CONTINENTAL AND ENGLISH TWIST TURNING

undoubtedly inferior, although they are more or less contemporary. The former is unquestionably by an English, and the latter by an alien craftsman. The other examples of marquetry (figs. 41 and 46) are also, judging from their high quality, from the hand of the foreign craftsman in England.

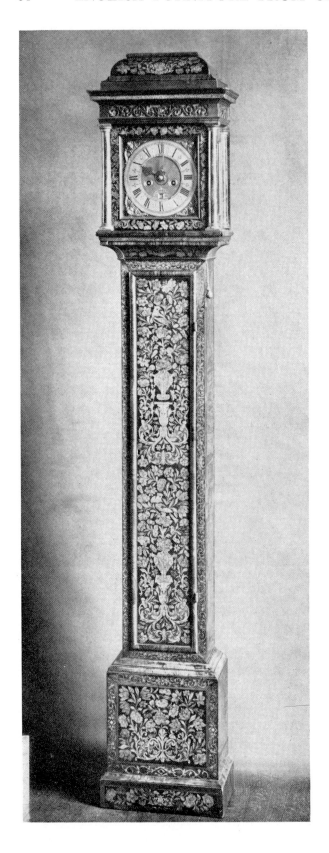

The woods used in marquetry were many and various. Evelyn, in his second edition of *Sylva*, published 1670, remarks :—" I know not whether it may be any Service to speak here of *Colour'd Woods*, I mean such as are naturally so, because besides the *Berbery* for *Yellow*, and *Holly* for *White*, we have very few : Our *Inlayers* use *Fustic*, *Locust*, or *Acacia* ; *Brasile*, *Prince* and *Rose-wood* for *Yellow* and *Reds*, with several others brought from both the *Indies* . . . ."

The light coloured woods were box, holly, sycamore, acacia and plane tree. Of box Evelyn says :—" . . . . the Roots of this *Tree* do furnish the *Inlayer* and *Cabinet-makers* with pieces rarely undulated, and full of variety." Referring to holly, he remarks that " The *Timber* of the Holly (besides that it is the Whitest of all hard *woods*, and therefore us'd by the *In-layer*, especially, under thin plates of *Ivory* to render it more conspicuous) is for all sturdy uses . . . ." Apple, pear, yew, bog oak and beech were also employed. Other natural coloured woods, not mentioned by Evelyn, were orange, citron, red sanders and sandal-wood.

In the floral marquetry, the petals of flowers and the veins of leaves, when made out of one piece of veneer, were portrayed by saw cuts which were accentuated by the glue which was forced through them in the process of laying the marquetry (fig. 42). Light coloured woods were shaded so as to

FIG. 48.—A SMALL LONG-CASE OR " GRANDMOTHER " CLOCK, DECORATED WITH FLORAL MARQUETRY, WITH EIGHT-DAY MOVEMENT BY CHRISTOPHER GOULD. HEIGHT, 5 FEET 8 INCHES.   CIRCA 1690.

give depth to the pattern by burning the surface of the veneer (figs. 41 and 42). How this was carried out, as described by Evelyn, has been quoted on page 43.

One widely mistaken belief with regard to marquetry is that the Dutch were the chief exponents of the floral variety on the Continent, and that the English copied it. This belief is mainly due to the large quantity of Dutch walnut furniture which is extant decorated with floral and bird inlay. This inlay is not marquetry in the sense that marquetry is inlaid work of which the pattern and the background are composed of veneers and cut together. It is also not contemporary with the piece it decorates, but has been added at a later date. The veneer on the piece which it is proposed to decorate is first cut out in the form of the inlay, which is then inserted and glued in position. This craze for ornamenting pieces by " chopping in " bird and floral marquetry came into vogue in Holland about 1820 and continued for at least fifty years, during which time a very large quantity of walnut veneered Dutch furniture of the seventeenth and eighteenth centuries, of pleasing design and good proportion, was ruined by this senseless act of nineteenth century

FIG. 19.—DETAIL SHOWING DIAL OF CLOCK, FIG. 18

FIG. 50.—DETAIL OF DRAWER SHOWING SQUARE-SHAPED ENGLISH LOCK.

FIG. 51.—DETAIL OF DRAWER SHOWING TALL RECTANGULAR-SHAPED LOCK PECULIAR TO FLEMISH AND FRENCH FURNITURE.

vandalism. The majority of this bird and floral inlay is of the coarsest workmanship, but there are examples of it which display greater care in the letting-in of the pattern, and, in such pieces, mother-o'-pearl is often used. The surface of many of these pieces, which have had the inlaid work executed eighty to one hundred years ago, will have acquired a patina so convincingly old that the inlay will have every appearance of being contemporary.

Judging from examples of furniture extant, the Dutch would appear to have used marquetry as a form of decoration in a lesser degree than the Germans, Flemings, and French. This especially applies to the floral marquetry which was a favourite variety with the French in the time of Louis XIII. and Louis XIV. It was also made in Flanders, which variety, as has already been stated, was copied by the English craftsmen. The French usually employed ebony for the background, while the Flemings more often used walnut, which they stained black. This has now faded to a deep brown colour. The Flemings, like the English, had a greater partiality for the oyster-shell veneer than the French, who did not use it to the same extent.

Pieces of French and Flemish floral marquetry nearly always have the tall lock to the drawers (fig. 51); whereas the Dutch furniture had the square lock similar to the English (fig. 50).

The Dutch in the seventeenth century made a type of marquetry which was very similar to the arabesque variety of the English. *Amorini* and grotesque heads in profile were often introduced into the design, which usually was of a light wood inlaid in a dark background, the former being shaded by hot sand. Judging from extant examples, however, the Dutch were far fonder of decorating their furniture with parquetry, composed of very elaborate oyster-shell veneers, often combined with ivory or bone inlay of geometrical design with stars.

PARQUETRY FURNITURE.

The ornamentation of furniture with oyster-shell parquetry, apart from its use in conjunction with marquetry, was much in vogue in the Stuart period of walnut. By

FIG. 52.—MIRROR WITH FRAME DECORATED WITH OYSTER-SHELL PARQUETRY OF OLIVE WOOD, AND ELABORATE CRESTING OF FOLIAGE CARVED IN SOFT WOOD ENCLOSING A CIPHER.   CIRCA 1685.   THIS MIRROR IS STRONGLY FRENCH IN CHARACTER.

Fig. 53.—TABLE WITH TOP VENEERED WITH LIGNUM VITÆ AND INLAID WITH GEOMETRICAL DESIGN IN HOLLY. THE CROSS GRAINED MOULDING TO TOP AND THE OYSTERSHELL VENEER ON THE DRAWER FRONT ARE OF OLIVE WOOD, AND THE LEGS ARE OF ELM. CIRCA 1670. FOR DETAIL, SEE FIG. 54.

FIG. 54.—DETAIL OF TOP OF TABLE, ILLUSTRATED FIG. 53.

the early years of the eighteenth century, it had gone out of fashion even in clock cases. This parquetry was made of oyster-shell veneer, each piece of which was carefully arranged to form a pattern on a table top, cabinet door or drawer front. Every piece of veneer was cut so that all the pieces fitted into each other, and they were then glued on to the carcase. Furniture decorated with parquetry often had the surfaces divided into geometrically shaped panels, either by thin lines of inlaid holly wood (fig. 54), or by cross-banded edgings, about ½ an inch in width, of a light wood, usually box or holly. Parquetry work was carried out in oyster-shell veneer of walnut, laburnum, olive, *lignum vitæ*, yew, cocus and kingwood. The last-named wood usually had the parquetry designed in the form of circles and spandrels, each piece of veneer forming a segment of the circle. Oyster veneer of kingwood is often found decorating the surrounds to seaweed marquetry panels in fine quality pieces of the William and Mary period (fig. 46). In such pieces the mouldings would also be cross-banded with kingwood.

The pieces usually found decorated with this oyster-shell parquetry are the oblong table with spiral or baluster turned legs (fig. 53), the chest-with-drawers, the long-case clock (fig. 55), the cabinet on stand with folding doors, lace boxes and mirror frames (fig. 52). Long-case parquetry clocks often had their doors and bases inlaid with stars and spandrels of holly (fig. 55).

In the Chandos sale catalogue "*A large lignum vitæ writing desk*" is mentioned. This may have been an example of a pedestal desk veneered with this type of oyster-shell parquetry.

Parquetry work of olive wood was specially favoured in the Stuart period. John Stalker, in his *Treatise of Japanning or Varnishing*, published 1688, refers to "Olive wood, which for Tables, Stands, Cabinets, &c, has been highly in request amongst us ; . . ."

Another type of parquetry work which, from examples extant, appears to have been in vogue in the reign of Queen Anne and up till as late as 1760, is a type of inlaid work composed of narrow strips of laburnum.* These strips are set at an acute angle to each other, thus forming a herring-bone pattern (fig. 57). The pieces most often found decorated with this type of parquetry are the early eighteenth century card table with the straight round leg ending in a club foot—similar to the walnut example illustrated (fig. 24), the pedestal dressing table, and small chests-with-drawers and pedestal writing tables ; rarer examples are chairs, tables and cabinets.

---

* Other woods that were used in this herring-bone parquetry were yew and fruit woods, such as cherry.

FIG. 55.—LONG-CASE CLOCK DECORATED WITH OLIVE WOOD PARQUETRY. MONTH MOVEMENT BY JOSEPH KNIBB, STRIKING ON TWO BELLS ACCORDING TO ROMAN NOTATION. CIRCA 1685.

WOODS USED FOR CARCASES AND DRAWER LININGS.

For the carcases of pieces throughout the walnut period, deal was generally used. An exception to this rule is the use of oak ; and it would appear that, from the examination of a large number of surviving examples, oak was chosen only for exceptional quality pieces, such pieces usually dating from the period of 1720-50, with perhaps the exception of fine marquetry examples of the William and Mary period. The reason for its employment was because the cabinet-makers considered it a superior wood to deal, and, when they made a fine quality piece, they used

FIG. 56.—DETAIL OF SKELETON DIAL OF CLOCK, FIG. 55.

it in preference. This, however, was not a general rule, as many pieces of the finest quality have deal carcases. It would appear, therefore, that oak was employed by certain cabinet-makers for their best quality pieces, and that an oak carcase to a walnut piece is always indicative that it is of superior quality. It should be noted in this respect, however, that the Dutch, unlike the English, almost always used oak for the carcasing of their walnut furniture, for both poor and fine quality examples. The reason for this was that deal was not an indigenous wood, and oak was, therefore, cheaper.

In the Stuart period, the English cabinet-maker appears seldom to have employed oak for the carcasing of his pieces. An interesting remark made by Evelyn about deal and oak in *Sylva* is : " I am sure we find it [Deal] an extraordinary saver of *Oak* where it may be had at reasonable price."

The deal that was used for the carcasing of walnut furniture was of the species known as the wild pine or the Scotch fir tree, generically called *Pinus Sylvestris*. This tree grew naturally in the Highlands of Scotland, and it also thrived in Denmark, Norway, and Sweden. Another quotation from *Sylva* referring to deal is : " I will not complain what an incredible mass of ready *Money* is yearly exported into the *Northern Countreys* for this sole Commodity, which might all be saved were we *industrious* at *home*." The timber of this Scotch fir tree was called deal, and it was sometimes of a reddish colour and sometimes yellow, but usually white. It was used not only for furniture, but also as a material for housebuilding and for the panelling of rooms, which last, in the seventeenth and early eighteenth century, was a very favourite treatment in all houses, except those of the lower classes.

A number of panelled rooms dating from the early eighteenth century are extant, made of this deal of the red colour variety. It is a good quality timber and free from knots. This last feature is specially noticeable when panelling of red deal is compared with that made from the white variety, which is full of knots and is a far inferior timber. For the carcasing of furniture, the yellow variety of deal appears mostly to have been used, as it is seldom found of red deal ; the colour of the carcases of pieces extant being a light tone, generally matured by age to an old ivory tint. This yellow deal was a superior timber to the white, free from knots and excellent as a ground for veneer. It is more than probable that, when they required the best timber, the cabinet-makers used the imported Continental variety, which was superior in quality to that which came from Scotland. Evelyn, in *Sylva*, writes about the fir tree : " Though *Whitenesse* be not the best *character ;* that which knowing *Workemen* call the *Dram*, and that comes to us from *Bergen, Swinfound, Mosse, Longlound, Dranton,* &c, long, strait, clear, and of a yellow more *Cedrie* colour, is esteemed much before the *White* for *flooring* and *wainscot ;* . . ''

Another variety of pine, *Picea Excelsa*, which is known as spruce, appears also to have been used at this period, but it is doubtful whether it was ever employed for furniture. Dr. Hunter, in his edition of Evelyn's *Sylva*, says : " This tree is common in the mountainous parts of Scotland, and in Norway, and affords the yellow deals." It is an inferior wood to the Scotch fir, and was used as a material for building.

Pepys, in his *Diary*, under date of 28th of September, 1666, makes mention of " deals " as regards building : " At night comes Sir W. Pen, and he and I a turn in the garden, and he broke to me a proposition of his and my joining in a design of fetching timber and deals from Scotland, by the help of Mr. Pett upon the place ; which, while London is building, will yield good money. I approve it." The re-building of London had been necessitated by the fire, which broke out on the 2nd August of that year.

Another variety of the pine tree, whose timber is superior in quality to that of the Scotch fir, is known as the Weymouth pine (*Pinus Strobus*). This tree was not indigenous to Europe during the first half of the eighteenth century ; in consequence, it was but seldom used for the carcases of walnut furniture. After about 1760, the cabinet-makers employed it for the carcases of mahogany and satinwood furniture of fine quality, because they found that it was a better wood than deal, its characteristics being that it was easier to work, and straight-grained, and had but little tendency to warp and shrink. This variety was called pine, and was not known as deal. Dr. Hunter makes the following reference to it in his edition of *Sylva* in 1776 :—" This grows naturally in most parts of North America . . . . The wood of this sort is esteemed for making masts for ships ; it is in England titled Lord Weymouth's, or New-England Pine . . . . there was a law made in the ninth year of Queen Ann for the preservation of the trees, and to encourage

Fig. 57.--Dressing Table with its original Toilet Mirror decorated with Parquetry of Laburnum. Circa 1745. This Table and Mirror are especially interesting, as it is seldom that an example of a Dressing Table has survived with its original Mirror The Handles are not original.

73

their growth in America ; and it is within these forty years that these trees began to be propagated in England in any plenty, though there were some large trees of this sort growing in two or three places long before, particularly at Lord Weymouth's, and Sir Wyndham Knatchbull's in Kent ; and it has been chiefly from the seeds of the latter that the much greater number of these trees now in England have been raised."

The distinguishing difference between yellow deal and pine, as regards the carcasing of furniture, is that when the unpolished surface of the latter matures by age it has a reddish cast. These two varieties, out of the many species of the pine tree, would appear to be the only two that were used in England for furniture making. Dr. Hunter writes : " This sort [Weymouth Pine] and the Scotch Pine are the best worth cultivating of all the kinds for the sake of their wood ; the others may be planted for variety in parks, &c."

For drawer linings, the cabinet-makers usually employed oak, as oak, being a hard wood, would be better able to withstand wear caused by friction, such as a drawer is subjected to in use.

Drawers belonging to the walnut furniture of the Stuart period usually have the drawer front of deal, and not of oak like the drawer linings. The reason for this was because the seventeenth century cabinet-makers found deal a better wood as a ground for veneer than oak, and, as the drawer front was veneered on the outside, they, in consequence, made it of deal. A remark of Evelyn, in *Sylva*, bears out this fact. Whilst discussing deal he writes : " nor does there any *Wood* so well agree with the *glew*, as it." The making of drawer fronts of deal in seventeenth century walnut furniture was by no means an invariable rule, as many examples will be found with the fronts of oak, but from pieces extant it would appear that the common practice was to use deal.

Sometimes a drawer with a deal front will be found to have the top edge covered with a strip of oak about ⅛ of an inch in thickness, so that the front has the appearance of being of oak. In eighteenth century walnut furniture, the drawer fronts were more often of oak, except in the case of lower grade pieces, when both the fronts and linings were made of deal. An exception to this is when the drawer bottom and front are of deal and the sides of oak. Drawer linings in walnut pieces will also be found of elm, ash, chestnut and beech, but such examples are generally the product of the country cabinet-maker.

Drawer linings made of Virginia walnut will be found on small walnut pieces of high quality, in which the drawers do not measure more than 2 feet 6 inches in width ; such pieces were the narrow bureau bookcase and the bureau on stand, also small chests-with-drawers. The small drawers in bureaux and toilet mirrors, and the boxes, trays and partitions of a fitted dressing-table drawer, were also usually made from this walnut. A few rare examples of the narrow bureau are extant with mahogany drawer linings ; this, however, was a very unusual feature.

The oak employed for the drawer linings of walnut pieces was generally of the highest quality. More often than not, it showed the medullary rays of the wood, denoting that it had been quarter cut. In many pieces the boards are wide, denoting that the timber was obtained from large trees. Evelyn, when writing about English oak in *Sylva*, says that

FIG. 58.—WALNUT DRESSING TABLE ON CABRIOLE LEGS OF UNUSUAL DESIGN.
CIRCA 1700.

it was " of much esteem in former times, till the finer grain'd *Norway* Timber came amongst us, which is likewise of a whiter colour." This, written in 1670, coupled with the fact that when oak is found in the construction of a walnut piece it is usually of the highest quality, gives weight to the presumption that the cabinet-makers used imported oak for their higher grade furniture. A feature about walnut furniture which displays a typical characteristic of the English craftsman, to " make a good job " of a piece, is that the interiors of cupboards and bookcases, when of good quality, will always be lined with a hard wood such as oak or walnut, and not a soft one like deal.

In a bureau bookcase, the carcase of the lower part will be of deal, as it is not seen except on the occasion of the removal of a drawer ; but the upper part will have the carcase forming the sides of oak, or walnut, as they are exposed to view upon opening the door. The central cupboard of kneehole dressing tables (figs. 59 and 60) will be lined with oak or walnut, and this is true of any cupboard in a walnut piece of good quality. The cabinet-makers realised that deal was a common wood as regards appearance, and they never allowed it to show, therefore, in a good quality piece. Pieces where this rule has been disregarded will, in the majority of cases, be found to be of poor quality, a fact which will be borne out by other signs of inferiority, both as regards workmanship and material.

Fig. 59.—WALNUT PEDESTAL DRESSING TABLE WITH LIFT-UP TOP DISCLOSING COMPARTMENT CONTAINING MIRROR AND FITTED TOILET BOXES. THIS TABLE WAS ONCE OWNED BY BYRON, THE POET, AND CAME FROM NEWSTEAD ABBEY. CIRCA 1735. IT IS AN OUTSTANDING EXAMPLE OF FINE QUALITY CRAFTSMANSHIP AND MATERIAL.

Fig. 60.—WALNUT PEDESTAL DRESSING TABLE.   CIRCA 1745.   THIS EXAMPLE IS LARGER THAN IS USUAL WITH THIS TYPE OF TABLE, AND ALSO HAS THE INTERESTING FEATURE OF A PULL-OUT SLIDE UNDER THE TOP, SUPPORTED BY LOPERS.   THE WALNUT TOILET MIRROR WITH ITS GILT GESSO FRAME IS CONTEMPORARY WITH THE TABLE.

The extravagant use of timber is a sign of quality in a chair. The more pronounced the curve of an arm or the rake of a back, the bigger the piece of timber will have to be from which it is cut, and the greater the waste, especially if the wood is used for one chair only. This is true of the chairs of both the Stuart and Georgian periods, in which the side rail to the back of a chair and the back leg are out of one piece. Many of the Stuart cane backed chairs of high quality would require a plank of walnut at least 10 inches in width from which to cut the back rail and leg, owing to the angle at which the rail joins the leg. In lower quality chairs, the back would be much more upright in order to economise in timber. The extravagant use of walnut in the Stuart period is especially interesting in view of the scarcity of the wood in England. Italian and French chairs of this period show an abundant use of timber, the arms being much more curved and the backs more raked ; and this is only to be expected, considering the plenitude of walnut in those countries.

CONSTRUCTION AND WORKMANSHIP.

The various methods of the construction of furniture in the walnut period and the quality of workmanship, are the next points to be considered.

One outstanding feature with regard to walnut furniture is that the furniture makers saved material at great trouble to themselves in the matter of construction and workmanship. By this is meant that they would employ a more elaborate construction, necessitating considerably more labour in the making of a piece, in order to economise in material ; the reason being that material was expensive and labour was cheap, exactly the reverse of what is the case to-day. This procedure also applied to mahogany furniture ; in fact, it was a ruling consideration throughout the eighteenth century, and in the seventeenth and first half of the eighteenth centuries was accentuated by reason of the still higher cost of timber.

DRAWERS.

Some of the most interesting changes in the methods of construction occur in connection with the dovetailing of drawers. Drawers in the majority of pieces up to the middle of the seventeenth century generally had the sides nailed to the drawer fronts and were hung on runners, as already explained. Drawers in fine quality buffets, dating from the Elizabethan period, and also the drawers of chests which had panelled fronts, sometimes inlaid with engraved bone decoration, usually had the drawer sides dovetailed with either one or two large dovetails to the drawer front (Diagram 2a).* The sides of the drawer were nailed to the back with large-headed hand-made nails. In the reign of Charles II., pieces of veneered walnut furniture had the drawer sides dovetailed both to the drawer front and the back. The dovetails fixing the sides to the front were wide, with coarse pin pieces (Diagram 2b). This method was known as " through " dovetailing, as the end grain of both the drawer front and sides were exposed, that of the drawer side being covered up by the veneer on the drawer front. This was unsatisfactory, as the end grain of the dovetail made a bad ground for the veneer especially if it was thin, when the dovetail joint would become visible. To obviate this defect the cabinet-makers adopted the

* Page 44

"lapped" or "stopped" dovetailing, in which the dovetail did not go through the drawer front, a lap being left upon the pin piece (Diagram 2c). It is difficult to give an approximate date to the introduction of this " lapped " dovetailing. Coarse examples of it have survived with wide dovetails and large pin pieces. Such examples point to a date between 1670-80, which would suggest that this type of dovetailing was nearly as early as the " through " type, the latter, however, being much more extensively used up to 1690. The " lapped " variety of dovetailing continued throughout the eighteenth century, the pin pieces becoming narrower and finer and the dovetails smaller and more in number as the century advanced (Diagram 2d). Fine quality pieces of walnut furniture of the last half of the Georgian period have the dovetailing to the drawers of the finest quality ; in fact, mahogany pieces of the late eighteenth century do not exhibit finer work.

Knowledge of dovetailing is of considerable value as it provides a great deal of information as to the date of a piece, and also, in many cases, is a reliable indication of its *provenance*.

Another point of interest as regards the construction of drawers, is the methods of fixing the drawer bottom to the sides. In the Jacobean oak furniture made before the accession of Charles II., the drawer bottoms were nailed on to the edge of the drawer sides, and the drawer hung on runners fixed to the carcase (Diagram 2a). A number of pieces of walnut furniture were made with the drawers hung in this manner, but examples are seldom found. It was a cumbersome method of construction, and one which the cabinet-makers must have quickly changed when they saw the advantage of a new method, which came in with the advent of veneered furniture. In this new type the runners were discarded, as the drawer rested on its bottom, the boards being flush with the lower edge of the drawer sides. A rabbet was cut into the drawer sides for the reception of the bottom (Diagram 2b). The boards were fixed in position by pins ; although a rarer method of fixing was by small wooden pegs inserted through the drawer sides. This, however, is seldom met with. The flush-bottom drawer, as this type is called, suffered from the disadvantage that, when it was opened and closed, the entire surface of the drawer bottom rubbed against the dust-board.

Towards the end of the seventeenth century, an improved method was introduced by which the drawer ran on runners fixed on its underside. In this type a deep rabbet was cut in the drawer side, so that it projected about $\frac{1}{4}$ of an inch below the drawer bottom. Butting against this projection, and equal in thickness to it, a narrow strip of wood was then glued on to the drawer bottom to act as a runner (Diagram 2c). A simpler and cheaper method was to do without the rabbet, nail the drawer bottom direct on to the underneath of the drawer sides, and glue on to it two narrow runners in the form of strips of wood flush with the drawer sides (Diagram 2b). Although this simpler method was very often employed, it is seldom found on pieces of high quality. This form of construction was also used without the runner being fixed on the bottom, there being a number of examples of this type extant (Diagram 2a). The addition of the runners may have been a later improvement that came in at the same time as the runners to the drawer with the rabbetted bottom.

Although the flush-bottom drawer went out of vogue at the end of the seventeenth century, it did so only in as far as the construction of large drawers was concerned. The drawers of small pieces of high quality, especially those with walnut linings, will often be found with this flush-bottom construction. This construction was nearly always used in the small drawers situated at the back of a bureau and in the drawers of toilet mirrors, both of walnut and mahogany.

In walnut furniture, it should be noted, the grain of the wood of a drawer bottom ran from back to front of the drawer : that is, parallel with the drawer sides (Diagrams 2*a*, *b*, *c*). Late pieces of walnut, however, will have the drawer bottoms running from side to side. There was considerable overlapping between the two methods, but it is seldom that a walnut piece earlier than 1740 is found with the drawer bottoms fixed in the latter manner. One exception to this may be found in narrow pieces with walnut or mahogany drawer linings, which usually have the grain of the drawer bottoms running from side to side.

Soon after the method of making drawers with the boards running from side to side had been adopted, cabinet-makers found that, in the case of long drawers, the bottom sagged. They therefore made the bottom in two parts with a muntin in the middle (Diagram 2*d*). This, however, is seldom found in walnut furniture, as it was a practice that was not followed until after the middle of the eighteenth century.

Among features peculiar to drawers, the following may be noted. The sides of those in Carolean walnut pieces, which are from $\frac{1}{4}$ to $\frac{3}{8}$ of an inch in thickness, had a square edge to the top (Diagram 2*a*). About 1680-90, the cabinet-makers started to round off this top edge (Diagrams 2*b*, *c*). At first it was done in a rather coarse manner, but about 1720 the drawer sides on good quality pieces became thinner, being sometimes under $\frac{1}{4}$ of an inch in thickness, with the top edge rounded in a more finished manner. Perfection in this respect was arrived at about 1725-40 in fine quality pieces, and especially examples with walnut drawer linings. The sides of the walnut-lined drawers were thin, particularly the small drawers of bureaux and those of toilet mirrors, which were sometimes only $\frac{1}{8}$ of an inch in thickness. The rounded top edge of such drawers was carefully finished ; the dovetails had narrow pin pieces, and the drawer bottoms were rabbetted, all displaying the highest quality craftsmanship. In fact, the quality of such small drawers in the Georgian school of walnut was exceptional, and in no way inferior to the cabinet-work of the mahogany-lined drawers of the satinwood furniture dating from about 1770 and later.

DUST-BOARDS.

Dust-boards, that is the horizontal divisions between the drawers, also show variation in their construction. The name " dust-board " is misleading. They were seldom fixed above the top drawer of a dressing-chest, which was fitted with toilet boxes and a mirror, the reason being, presumably, that this type of drawer was invariably fixed so that it could not be taken out. There was, therefore, no necessity to fit a board between it and the underneath drawer, as the contents of the latter could not be got at through the opening of the one above it. This seems to imply that these boards were fitted solely for the purpose of protecting the contents of the drawers from being stolen or tampered with, and not to protect them from dust.

In walnut furniture of the Stuart school, these boards were composed of wide pieces of deal about ½ an inch in thickness and shot jointed, and were housed in the sides of the carcase. The front edge was usually veneered with the half-round cross-grained moulding, typical of the early period of Stuart walnut furniture, and the back edge, in the majority of examples, was 2 to 3 inches away from the back board of the piece, in some cases being short by as much as 8 to 10 inches. The reason for this was that the cabinet-maker was economising in material. Such a type of dust-board is known as the " full bottom " (Diagram 4*a, b*).

About 1680-90, the construction of these dust-boards was altered. A front rail, usually about 1½ to 3 inches in width, was fitted. The dust-board, made of a thinner plank of wood, was then fixed to this rail, the two ends being housed in the carcase sides as before (Diagram 4*c, d*). In this method of construction the top of the rail and the dust-board were flush ; but, as the rail was thicker than the board, it projected below it on the underneath side. This would cause the drawer, when open, to dip downwards, and, in order to avoid this, two narrow strips of wood were often fixed under the dust-board abutting on to the sides of the carcase, so that it became the same thickness as the front rail above the sides of the drawer, thus preventing the drawer from dipping when opened. The construction of this kind of dust-board entailed considerably more labour, and the only advantages were the economy that could be effected through using a thinner piece of timber, and the reduction of weight. A dust-board of this type usually went through to the back, which the cabinet-maker could afford to do with the thinner wood. Sometimes the front rail may be found to be of oak, and, in superior quality pieces, the dust-boards themselves will be of oak, in which case the carcase can be expected to be of the same wood.

Dutch furniture will not be found fitted with this last type of dust-board. The divisional rail will be present, but not the board. Fine quality Dutch examples, especially those dating from the eighteenth century, will sometimes be found with the full-bottom board, similar to the Stuart walnut examples. Such boards, however, will be of oak and not of deal, and also seldom extend to the back. The fact that a piece is not fitted with a dust-board is not invariably a sign of foreign *provenance*, as country-made walnut pieces will be found more often than not with the division rail only. The cabinet-maker was here following out the traditions of the Jacobean school.

MOULDINGS AND BANDINGS.

One of the outstanding features of walnut furniture is the cross-grained mouldings. By this is meant that the grain of the wood runs across the width of the moulding and not along its length. Such mouldings were made before they were applied to the piece. They were formed by gluing thin pieces of walnut, with the grain running crossways, on to a deal core. The surface of the walnut was then given the desired section by being planed with a moulding plane, the iron of which was shaped inversely to the section required.

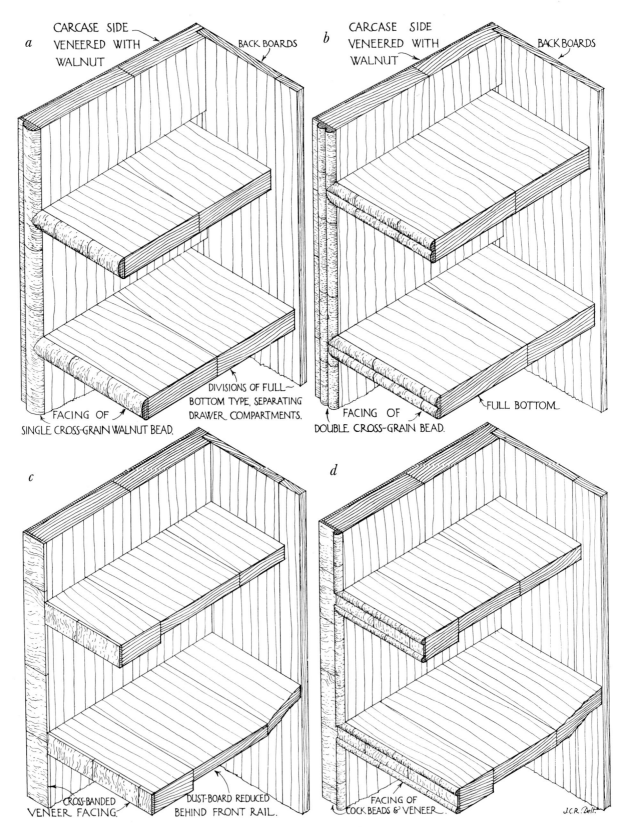

a
CARCASE SIDE VENEERED WITH WALNUT
BACK BOARDS
FACING OF SINGLE CROSS-GRAIN WALNUT BEAD.
DIVISIONS OF FULL-BOTTOM TYPE, SEPARATING DRAWER COMPARTMENTS.

b
CARCASE SIDE VENEERED WITH WALNUT
BACK BOARDS
FACING OF DOUBLE CROSS-GRAIN BEAD.
FULL BOTTOM

c
CROSS-BANDED VENEER FACING.
DUST-BOARD REDUCED BEHIND FRONT RAIL.

d
FACING OF COCK BEADS & VENEER.

J.C.R. Delt.

Diagram 4.—DETAILS SHOWING MOULDINGS SURROUNDING DRAWER FRONTS AND CONSTRUCTION OF DUST-BOARDS.

H

82

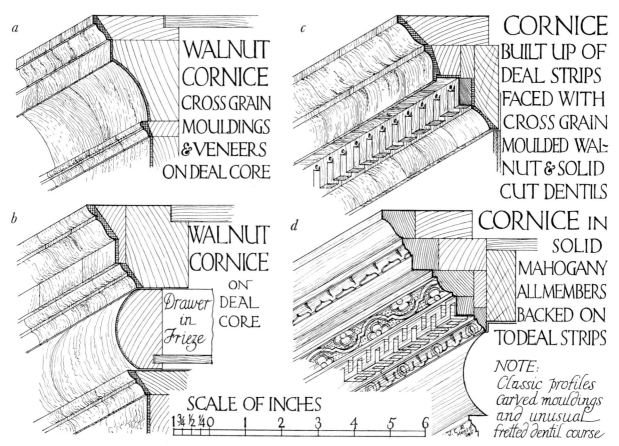

Diagram 5.—DETAILS SHOWING SECTIONS AND METHODS OF CONSTRUCTION OF CORNICES OF WALNUT AND MAHOGANY FURNITURE.

Cornices which had large members, such as the *cavetto* or the bulbous moulding, in their section had these portions veneered with cross-grained walnut (Diagram 5*a* and *b*). Cornices with a *corona*, that is, a square projection, will also be found to have the surfaces veneered (Diagram 5*c* and fig. 63). A sign of high quality in a *corona* cornice is when the soffit is recessed, thus forming a drip mould (Diagram 5*c*). Such a detail as this would increase the cost, as it entails considerably more work. The examination of mouldings will reveal much information concerning the quality of a piece. To see the true section of a moulding, the profile where it returns on a corner should be examined and not the straight run of the moulding, where the actual section can never be accurately gauged.

In Carolean furniture, the mouldings are coarse and of rather a shallow section. The cabinet-makers, being unskilled in working cross-grained mouldings, did not attempt elaborate sections with intricate members, like those belonging to the Georgian walnut period, when the craftsman had achieved a far higher competence. In this latter period the mouldings were of a more accentuated section, denoting that he had become more skilled in the use of the moulding plane.

An unusual and rare feature denoting fine workmanship, only to be found on superlative quality pieces of the Georgian walnut school, is when the cock beads to a drawer

Fig. 61.—WALNUT CABINET WITH MOULDINGS AND SCROLL PEDIMENT TOP OF MAHOGANY.   CIRCA 1735.
THE INTERIOR OF THIS CABINET IS FITTED WITH A SECRETAIRE, PIGEON HOLES AND DRAWERS.

84

Fig. 62.—Walnut Bookcase with Mirror Doors.   Circa 1750.   The Fret Ornament to the Frieze is
An Unusual Feature on Walnut Furniture.   For Detail, see Fig. 63.

85

FIG. 63.—DETAIL OF CORNICE SHOWING APPLIED FRET FRIEZE OF WALNUT BOOKCASE, FIG. 62.

are made of cross-grained walnut. Such a refinement as this necessitated a great deal of extra labour and skill, the usual method being to form the cock beads from straight run walnut. Sometimes the cock bead which is fixed around the drawer opening (Diagram 4d) will be found of cross-grained wood. The overlapping drawer edge will also be found of cross-grained walnut as well as of straight run walnut. A cross-grained moulding of this design is by no means so rare a feature as the cross-grained cock bead. In a fine quality bureau, the partitions forming the pigeon holes and those between the small drawers will have the edges of cross-grained walnut ; in the more ordinary examples the edges will be rounded only.

Sometimes a piece of poor quality will have the ovolo moulding worked on the edge of a solid drawer front, in which case it will not overlap. An analogous example to this is the " scratch " bead, which is scratched on the surface of the front. This simpler and cheaper method of forming a cock bead is often found employed in mahogany furniture dating from 1730-50, in which the drawers have solid fronts. A number of veneered walnut examples are extant with the beads scratched on the surface of the veneer.

Another sign of quality as regards mouldings is when the walnut, of which they are composed, has a finely marked figure. Mouldings of olive and kingwood furniture are specially noteworthy in this respect. On poor quality and cheap pieces the mouldings on the sides will sometimes be found of deal, only the mouldings on the front being of cross-grained walnut. On such pieces, the veneer on the sides will also be omitted, the deal carcase being stained to imitate walnut. Such examples are generally chests-with-drawers, bureaux and tallboys dating from the Georgian period.

Throughout the walnut period, the cabinet-makers treated a surface such as a drawer front, the top of a chest-with-drawers, the fall of a bureau, secretaire, and a table top, as a panel framed by a border. In the Stuart school of walnut, the borders were of various types. In the Carolean period, they generally took the form of a band of veneer in which the grain ran across the width : this is known as a cross-banded edging (fig. 54). Sometimes there were one or two narrow lines of inlaid holly dividing this edging from the central panel of veneer. Oyster-shell parquetry pieces were often framed by a ½ inch band of inlaid holly or box (fig. 41). Another favourite type of border edging, known as the herring-bone or feather inlay, was made of two strips of cross-banded veneer cut with the grain on the slant. The strips were laid side by side so that the grain formed an acute angle. This herring-bone band was sometimes used as an inner border to the cross-banded edging (fig. 66), but, on smaller surfaces such as drawer fronts, was sometimes used alone. In Carolean examples, it was wider than in those of a later date. In the Georgian school of walnut, it was extensively used on all types of furniture, sometimes with the cross-banded edging and sometimes without. An alternative but rarer type of inlaid band used in the Georgian walnut period was a checker design formed of minute squares and rectangles of light and dark coloured inlay (figs. 61 and 85).

The sides of pieces of furniture were seldom, even in good quality pieces, decorated with more than a cross-banded edging, and this generally on the front and back edges only. Sometimes a very fine quality piece had the sides bordered with a band of herring-bone inlay contained in a cross-banded edging. This, however, was extremely unusual ; see detail drawing of walnut bureau bookcase (Diagram 6). In lower quality pieces, the sides were without any bandings whatsoever.

CARVING.

The remaining factor to be considered with regard to quality of workmanship is carving. With carving, the shaping and moulding of a plain member, such as an arm or the leg of a chair, must also be included, because, although plain and undecorated, it owes its feeling and outline to the tool of the carver (fig. 74). This question of shape and form is of great importance to the student of walnut furniture, especially so far as chairs are concerned, as the intrinsic merit of such pieces is by no means dependent upon carving, which, as already explained in the previous chapter, is only of value from an ornamental and superficial point of view.

Throughout the walnut period, carving, either in the form of shaping and moulding plain pieces or as decoration, plays but little part except in chairs, stools, settees and the legs of tables and stands. It was seldom that the cabinet-maker required the assistance of the carver in making veneered furniture ; but, with the chair-maker, it was entirely different, as every part of his design was dependant upon the shape given to it by the spoke-shave or chisel. Carving is far more dependant upon the individual skill of the crafts-man than the veneered work of the cabinet-maker, and, unless the former has been guided by tradition and the practice of years, and has worked in the same slowly and imper-ceptibly changing style, his work will lack the spirit and character of his own time. The carver's work is instinct with a feeling which it is difficult to show accurately on a full size working drawing. Much must always be left to the workman's instinctive sense as to what is right. Unless endowed with this feeling, no work will possess that essential subtlety, and thereby distinction, which comes from saturation in the spirit, and therefore

Fig. 64.—Walnut bureau bookcase with burr veneer on the front, and straight-grained veneer on the sides. Circa 1740. The drawer linings are of Virginia walnut, and the carved enrichment of lime wood gilt. For details see figs. 65, 66 and 67, and measured drawings Diagrams 6 and 7. This piece is of outstanding quality in all respects.

FIG. 65.—DETAIL OF CORNICE AND PEDIMENT, SHOWING CARVED ORNAMENT IN GILT LIME WOOD, OF WALNUT BUREAU BOOKCASE, FIG. 64.

full understanding of the style of the period to which the design belongs. There is no universal style to-day, and therefore no such distinction (one might paradoxically say no originality), while the craftsman no longer possesses the instinctive sense without which he is but a machine. The old craftsmen, on the contrary, contributed to any given design an intuitive interpretation of the style of the period in which they lived. Such craftsmen were able to take liberties with a design and yet remain correct. They would make one arm of a chair slightly different in its dimensions from the other. They would also give one arm a more accentuated curve ; and yet, despite these discrepancies, or perhaps because of them, their chairs will be full of grace and harmony, since these inaccuracies are as characteristic of hand-made work as accuracy and precision are inseparable from machine work. Their instinct would never permit them to commit a fault that would be noticeable or appear wrong. Compare this with the modern workman reproducing an antique chair. The presence of the original by his side and the closest measurements will prevent him from going astray. But, if he should take the slightest licence, or if he has only working drawings to go upon, then a small percentage of error will creep

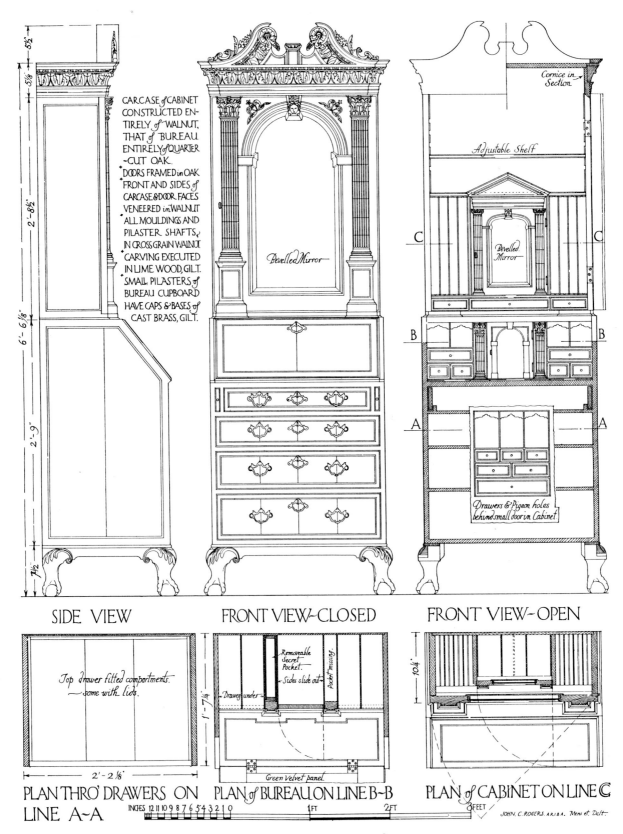

CARCASE of CABINET
CONSTRUCTED EN-
TIRELY of WALNUT,
THAT of BUREAU
ENTIRELY of QUARTER
-CUT OAK.
DOORS FRAMED in OAK
FRONT AND SIDES of
CARCASE & DOOR FACES
VENEERED in WALNUT
ALL MOULDINGS AND
PILASTER SHAFTS,
IN CROSS GRAIN WALNUT.
CARVING EXECUTED
IN LIME WOOD, GILT.
SMALL PILASTERS of
BUREAU CUPBOARD
HAVE CAPS & BASES of
CAST BRASS, GILT.

Bevelled Mirror

Cornice in Section

Adjustable Shelf

Bevelled Mirror

Drawers & Pigeon holes behind small door in Cabinet

SIDE VIEW

FRONT VIEW~CLOSED

FRONT VIEW~OPEN

*Top drawer fitted compartments.
— some with lids.*

Removeable Secret Pocket.

Sides slide out

Pocket missing

Drawers under

Green Velvet panel

PLAN THRO' DRAWERS ON
LINE A~A

PLAN of BUREAU ON LINE B~B

PLAN of CABINET ON LINE C

INCHES 12 11 10 9 8 7 6 5 4 3 2 1 0   1 FT   2 FT   3 FEET

JOHN. C. ROGERS. A.R.I.B.A. Mens et Delt.

Diagram 6.—MEASURED DRAWING OF WALNUT BUREAU BOOKCASE, FIG. 64.

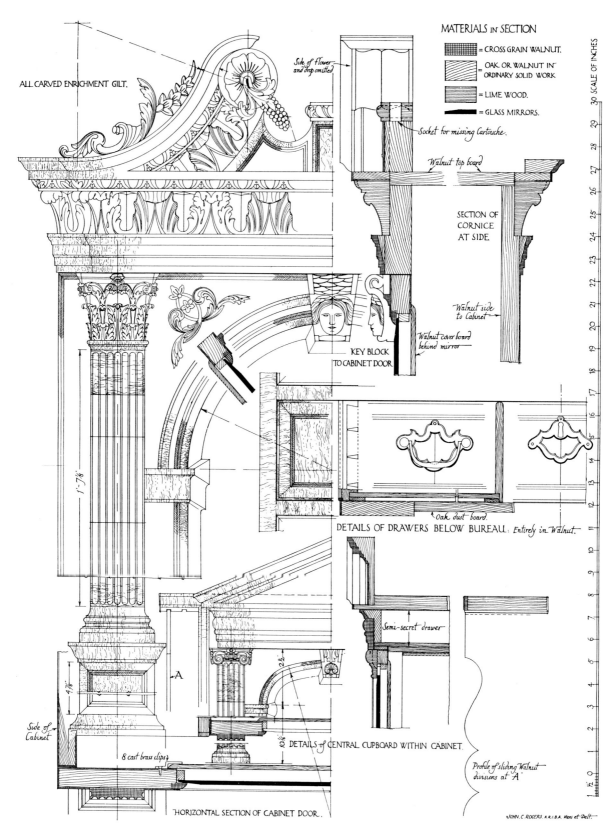

MATERIALS in SECTION

▓▓▓ = CROSS GRAIN WALNUT.

▨▨▨ = OAK OR WALNUT IN ORDINARY SOLID WORK

▦▦▦ = LIME WOOD.

▬▬▬ = GLASS MIRRORS.

ALL CARVED ENRICHMENT GILT.

Side of flower and drip omitted

Socket for missing Cartouche.

Walnut top board

SECTION OF CORNICE AT SIDE

Walnut side to Cabinet

Walnut cover board behind mirror

KEY BLOCK TO CABINET DOOR

1'-7⅜"

DETAILS OF DRAWERS BELOW BUREAU: Entirely in Walnut.

Oak dust board.

A

4⅛"

Side of Cabinet

8 cast brass clips

Semi-secret drawer

2½"

10⅜"

DETAILS OF CENTRAL CUPBOARD WITHIN CABINET.

Profile of sliding Walnut divisions at 'A'

HORIZONTAL SECTION OF CABINET DOOR.

JOHN. C. ROGERS. A.R.I.B.A. Mens et Delt.

30 SCALE OF INCHES

Diagram 7.—MEASURED DRAWING SHOWING DETAILS OF WALNUT BUREAU BOOKCASE, FIG. 64.

91

into the design, which will not be consonant with the spirit of eighteenth century work, because he will lack the instinctive sense of the man who made the original chair.

There is considerable variation in carving from the coarsest to the finest. There is, however, but little in common between the carving of the Stuart and the Georgian periods. In the former, the carved ornament on the chairs of 1660 was coarse and in low relief. From this date up to the reign of William and Mary a gradual evolution of refinement took place until, in the latter period, it was very highly finished indeed, in high relief, and of an open-work character. Contemporary Continental chairs of high grade display the highest quality carving throughout this period, but it was not until 1690 that the English craftsman succeeded in acquiring a skill similar to that of his foreign *confrère*.

In the Georgian school, the carved decoration was of a different character. There was no open-work in the design ; it was restrained, and a fine and discriminating taste was displayed in its use. It is in this period that there was considerable ·variation in the degree of quality, which varied between the superlative, the mediocre and the coarse. Walnut was not as good a medium for carving as mahogany, and the finest quality carving in the former wood does not reach the same level of perfection as that in mahogany. Walnut is a softer wood than mahogany, and, in consequence the carving lacks virility and the sculpturesque effect which are the outstanding features of carved ornament in mahogany.

FIG. 66.—DETAIL OF FOOT OF WALNUT BUREAU BOOKCASE, FIG. 64.

The character of the Stuart school of ornament was far more suitable for walnut than that of the Georgian period. An exception to this is the very low relief carving found on chairs of the latter period. This type of carved ornament was far more frequently used in conjunction with walnut furniture than with mahogany. The ornament is executed in very low relief from a thin layer of wood, which was afterwards glued on to the top of the veneer, when it had the appearance of having been carved out of the solid (fig. 73).

The acanthus leaf foliage decorating the knees of cabriole legs, when executed in a hard wood, such as mahogany, permitted the carver to give an elaboration of florid detail, the leaves intertwining with each other in well-defined and graceful scrolls. To carry out such a design in walnut is

FIG. 67.—INTERIOR OF BUREAU BOOKCASE, ILLUSTRATED FIG. 64.

Fig. 68.—WALNUT BUREAU DRESSING TABLE, 2 FEET $3\frac{1}{2}$ INCHES IN WIDTH.   CIRCA 1735.   THIS IS A VERY UNUSUAL EXAMPLE, OWING TO THE LEGS BEING DECORATED WITH THE LION MASK MOTIF.   THE FRONT IS VENEERED WITH BURR WALNUT, AND THE DRAWERS ARE LINED WITH VIRGINIA WALNUT.   ORIGINALLY, THIS BUREAU WAS SURMOUNTED WITH A TOILET GLASS.   FOR DETAIL, SEE FIG. 70.

94

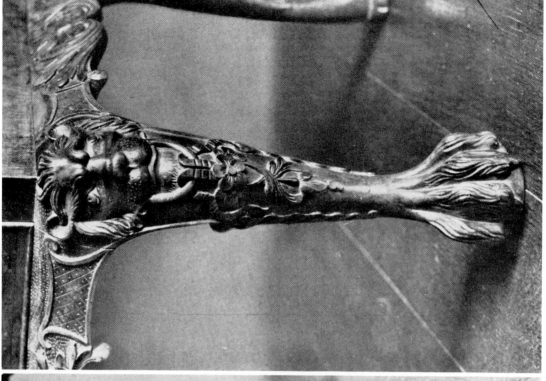

FIG. 70.—DETAIL OF LION MASK MOTIF, WITH RING, ON LEG OF WALNUT DRESSING BUREAU, FIG. 68.

95

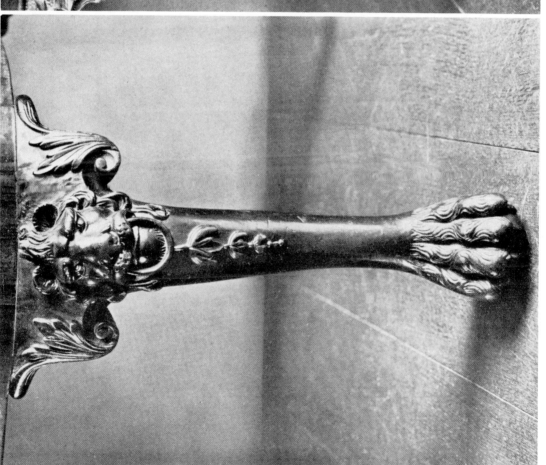

FIG. 69.—DETAIL OF LION MASK MOTIF, WITH RING, ON LEG OF MAHOGANY CHAIR, FIG. 135.

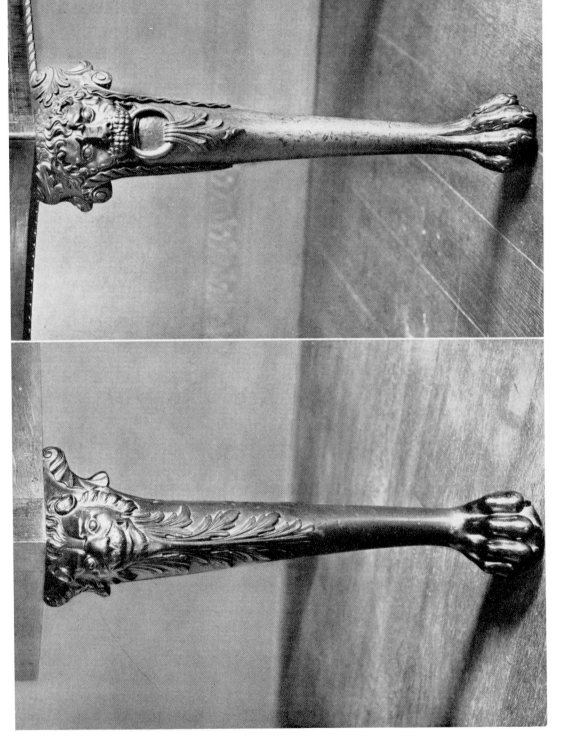

FIG. 71.—DETAIL OF ANIMAL MASK MOTIF, ON LEG OF MAHOGANY
TABLE, FIG. 127.

FIG. 72.—DETAIL OF LION MASK MOTIF, WITH RING, ON WALNUT CARD
TABLE, FIG. 34.

Fig. 83.—SCONCE WITH WALNUT FRAME ENCLOSING PANEL OF
PETIT-POINT NEEDLEWORK.   CIRCA 1715.

113

Fig. 84.—WALNUT BUREAU DRESSING TABLE. CIRCA 1725.
A VERY UNUSUAL FEATURE OF THIS PIECE IS THAT THE DRAWER LININGS ARE OF MAHOGANY.
THE INSIDE OF THE BUREAU IS IDENTICAL WITH THAT OF EXAMPLE ILLUSTRATED FIG. 85.

114

Fig. 85.—Walnut Writing Bureau.   Circa 1725.   The drawer linings of this piece are of mahogany, see illustration, Fig. 84.   An unusual feature are the turned wood knob handles, which are original. This bureau was never fitted with a toilet mirror similar to the example illustrated Fig. 84.

FIG. 86.—WINGED ARMCHAIR WITH WALNUT LEGS AND ORIGINAL GROS-POINT NEEDLEWORK COVERING.   C. 1720.
THE BACK OF THIS CHAIR IS MADE TO RAISE AND LOWER BY MEANS OF A RATCHET.

Fig. 87.—Winged armchair with walnut legs and petit-point needlework covering.   circa 1730

117

Fig. 88.—Winged armchair with walnut and gilt legs, and petit and gros-point needlework covering.
Circa 1740

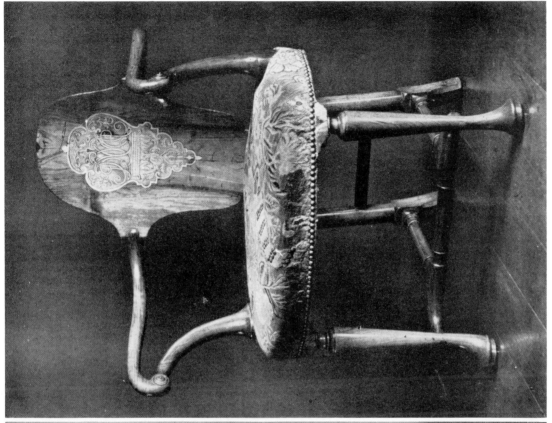

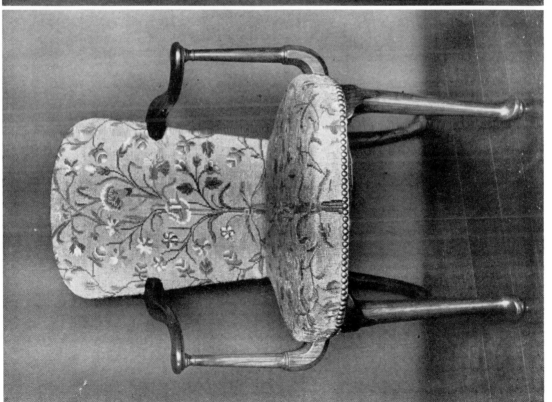

Fig. 90.—Walnut writing chair with oval seat, and back decorated with panel of marquetry containing cipher of the Dudley North family (Fig. 47). Circa 1715. The back legs of this chair are of beech.

Fig. 89.—Armchair of chestnut with petit-point needlework covering. Circa 1715.

119

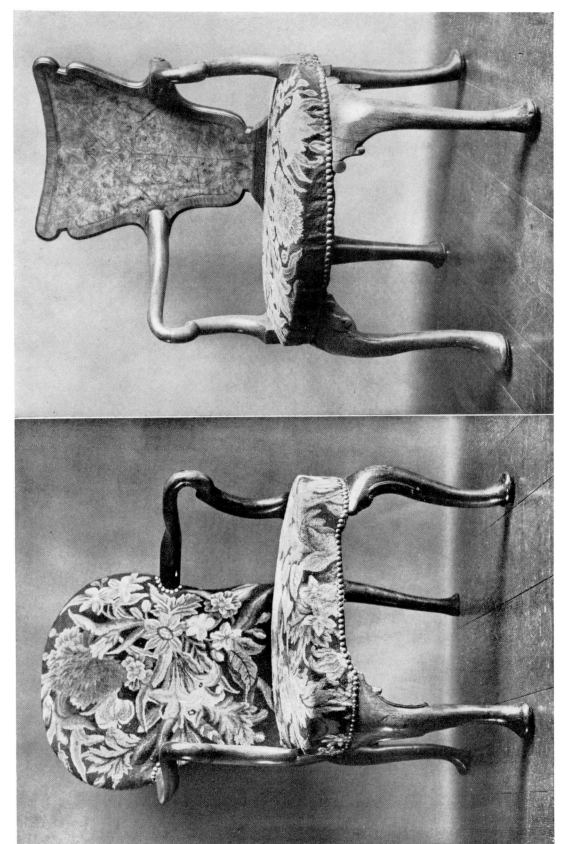

Fig. 91.—Walnut armchair with petit-point needlework covering. One of a pair. Circa 1730.

Fig. 92.—Walnut writing chair with oval seat, and back of burr veneer. Circa 1725.

120

FIG. 93.—ONE OF A PAIR OF WRITING CHAIRS WITH BACK AND SEAT RAIL   FIG. 94.—ONE OF A PAIR OF WALNUT WRITING CHAIRS.

OF BURR WALNUT VENEER, AND LEGS AND ARMS OF ELM.   CIRCA 1730.   CIRCA 1725.

121

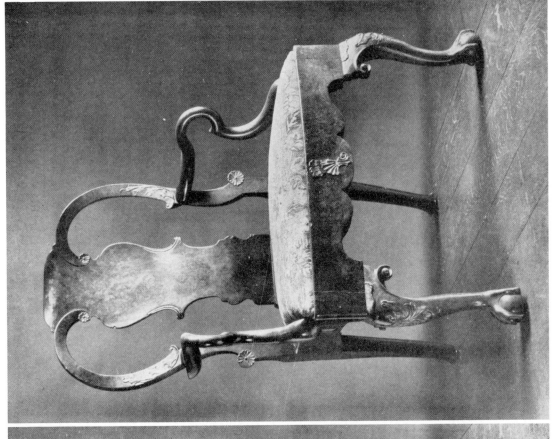

FIG. 95.—WALNUT ARMCHAIR WITH BACK AND SEAT RAIL OF BURR VENEER. CIRCA 1730. FOR DETAIL, SEE FIG. 19.

FIG. 96.—WALNUT ARMCHAIR WITH SHALLOW CARVED DECORATION APPLIED ON TO THE SURFACE OF THE VENEER. CIRCA 1735. FOR DETAIL, SEE FIG. 74.

122

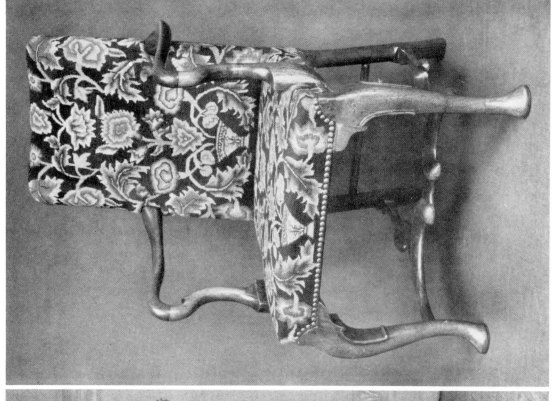

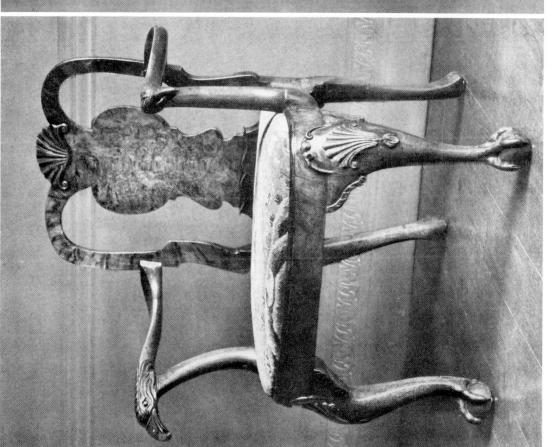

FIG. 97.—WALNUT ARMCHAIR WITH FOUNDATION TO THE SPLAT OF BEECH OVERLAID
WITH BURR VENEER.   CIRCA 1725.   FOR DETAIL, SEE FIG. 14.

FIG. 98.—WALNUT ARMCHAIR COVERED WITH ORIGINAL PETIT-POINT
NEEDLEWORK.   THE STRETCHER IS OF UNUSUAL DESIGN.   CIRCA 1720.

123

FIG. 99.—MAHOGANY WRITING CHAIR.   CIRCA 1735.   THIS CHAIR DESIGNED WITH THREE LEGS IN FRONT AND
ONE AT THE BACK, AND WITH A CRESTING INCORPORATING THE TUDOR ROSE, IS OF OUTSTANDING INTEREST.
IT ALSO RESEMBLES THE FIVE-LEGGED CHAIR ILLUSTRATED, FIG. 100.

FIG. 100.—WRITING CHAIR OF ELM, OF UNUSUAL DESIGN, WITH FIVE LEGS.   THE BACK AND SEAT RAIL ARE OF
ELM VENEER.   CIRCA 1735.

125

FIGS. 101 AND 102.—TWO WALNUT ARMCHAIRS WITH PETIT-POINT NEEDLEWORK COVERING.   CIRCA 1745.

126

FIG. 103.—BEECH STOOL, POLISHED BLACK.   CIRCA 1695.
FIG. 104.—WALNUT STOOL.   CIRCA 1685.

127

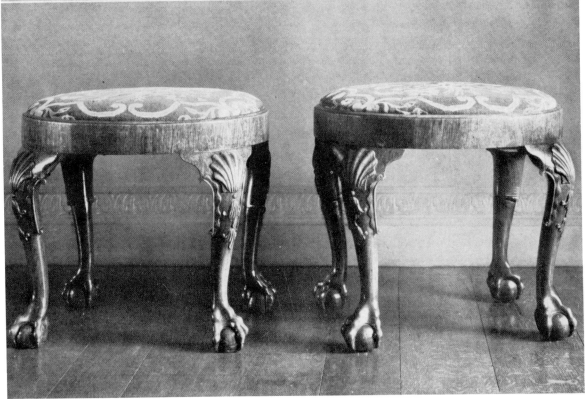

FIG. 105.—PAIR OF CIRCULAR WALNUT STOOLS.   CIRCA 1685.

FIG. 106.—PAIR OF OVAL WALNUT STOOLS.   CIRCA 1735.

Fig. 107.—WALNUT CLOSE STOOL.   CIRCA 1725.   THIS EXAMPLE IS OF AN UNUSUAL DESIGN, THE LID
OF THE STOOL BEING FORMED OF TWO DUMMY VOLUMES OF BOOKS.

Fig. 108.—WALNUT CLOSE STOOL.   CIRCA 1715.   THE TURNED LEGS OF THIS STOOL, WHICH ARE
TYPICAL OF THE FURNITURE OF THE GEORGE I PERIOD, ARE SIMILAR TO THE LEGS OF THE WRITING CHAIR
ILLUSTRATED FIG. 90.

129

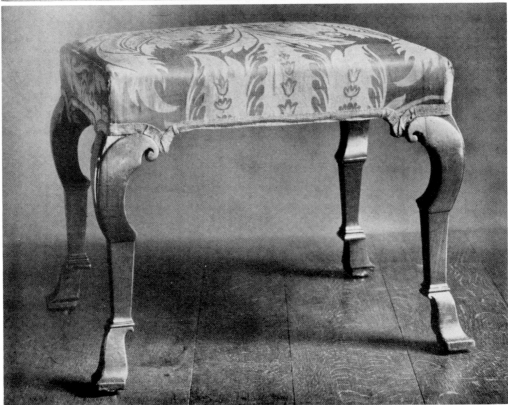

FIG. 109.—OVAL WALNUT STOOL   CIRCA 1725.
FIG. 110.—WALNUT STOOL.   CIRCA 1715.

130

FIG. 111.—WALNUT STOOL.   CIRCA 1740.
FIG. 112.—WALNUT STOOL.   CIRCA 1735.

131

FIG. 113.—WALNUT STOOL.   CIRCA 1740.
FIG. 114.—WALNUT STOOL.   CIRCA 1730.

FIG. 115.—WALNUT BACHELOR CHEST WITH FOLDING TOP. CIRCA 1715. FIG. 116.—WALNUT BACHELOR CHEST WITH FOLDING TOP. CIRCA 1720. THESE CHESTS ARE TERMED TO-DAY "BACHELOR CHESTS"; THERE APPEARS TO BE NO WRITTEN EVIDENCE, HOWEVER, THAT THEY WERE SO CALLED IN THE EIGHTEENTH CENTURY.

133

FIG. 118.—WALNUT PEDESTAL DRESSING TABLE WITH CANTED CORNERS.
BOTH CIRCA 1730.

FIG. 117.—WALNUT PEDESTAL DRESSING TABLE.

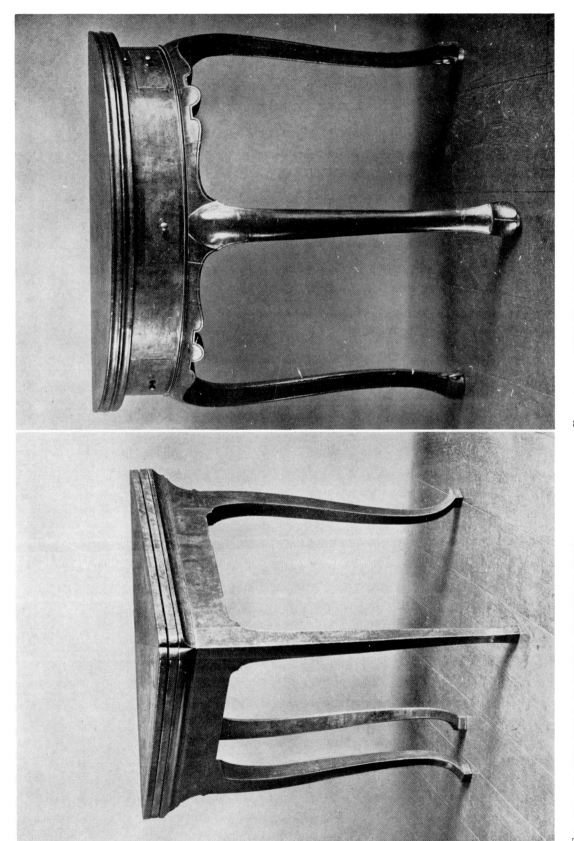

FIG. 120.—WALNUT CARD TABLE WITH FRIEZE AND TOP OF BURR VENEER. CIRCA 1705.

FIG. 119.—WALNUT TABLE OF UNUSUAL TRIANGULAR SEAPE. CIRCA 1710.

135

136

M

FIG. 123.—WALNUT TOILET MIRROR OF UNUSUALLY LARGE DIMENSIONS, WITH
BUREAU IN BASE. CIRCA 1725. THE DRAWER IS FITTED WITH TOILET
BOXES AND COMPARTMENTS MADE OF VIRGINIA WALNUT.

FIG. 124.—WALNUT TOILET MIRROR. CIRCA 1710. THE EARLY SCROLL
FOOT TO THIS MIRROR IS AN UNUSUAL FEATURE.

137

CHAPTER III.

MAHOGANY FURNITURE,

1720-60.

THE introduction of mahogany, unlike walnut, did not coincide with a new style in furniture. Its use at first was gradual, as it failed to oust walnut in the same manner as walnut supplanted oak. A well-known story, which is undoubtedly based on actual fact, concerning its first use by a cabinet-maker in England, is quoted here at length from a work entitled *A Book of English Trades*, published in the year 1821 :—

"The first use to which mahogany was applied in England, was to make a box for holding candles. Dr. [William] Gibbons, an eminent physician, at the latter end of the seventeenth century, had a brother, a West-India captain, who brought over some planks of this wood as ballast. As the Doctor was then building a house in King-Street, Covent Garden, his brother thought they might be of service to him ; but the carpenters finding the wood too hard for their tools, they were laid aside as useless. Soon after, Mrs. Gibbons wanting a candle-box, the Doctor called on his Cabinet-maker (Wollaston, of Long-Acre) to make him one of some wood that lay in the garden. The candle-box was made, and approved ; and the Doctor then insisted on having a bureau made of the same wood, which was accordingly done ; and the fine colour, polish, &c., were so pleasing, that his friends were invited to come and see it. Amongst whom was the Duchess of Buckingham [Mary Fairfax, wife of George Villiers, 2nd Duke of Buckingham]. Her Grace begged some of the wood of Dr. Gibbons, and Wollaston made her a bureau also ; on which the fame of the mahogany, and Mr. Wollaston, was raised, and things of this kind became general."

The outstanding difference between mahogany and walnut is that mahogany is a heavier, a more close-grained, and a harder wood. Because of the last-named quality it was easily given a high polish, and this, together with its reddish tint, resulted in a richness of effect which must have seemed extremely attractive when furniture was first made from it, contrasting as it did so strongly with the golden brown tone of walnut. Not only was mahogany a wood of superior quality in comparison with walnut, as it had little tendency to warp or twist, but planks of it could be obtained of much greater width than was possible with walnut. Another asset possessed by mahogany was its freedom from attack by the worm, which was always liable to mine walnut. It was also a much stronger wood, a quality which the chair makers quickly realised, as it permitted them to make the legs, rails and backs of their chairs more slender in form and with more accentuated curves than was possible with walnut. Yet another feature of mahogany was that, although it was a much harder wood than walnut, it was an excellent medium for carving, mention of which has already been made on page 92. Against these qualities in favour of mahogany must be reckoned the fact that it lacked the fine figure and the marking of walnut. This, however, applies only to the San Domingo or Spanish mahogany, which was the first variety to be used in cabinet-making. Mahogany of fine figure was employed by the cabinet-makers, about 1750-60, when the varieties known as Cuban and Honduras began to be imported.

DESIGN.

Mahogany affected the design of furniture because, as has already been pointed out, logs of it could be obtained of bigger bulk than was possible with walnut, and because, being a plain wood with little marking, the furniture was accordingly made in the solid. This plainness also caused a greater use of carving as a means of ornamentation.

The fact that the wood could be obtained in wider planks particularly affected the design of tables. In the walnut period, dining tables must undoubtedly have always presented a difficulty to the cabinet-makers, owing to the fact that both English and Virginia walnut could not be obtained of sufficient width to make the wide leaf of a table top out of one plank.

Tables with tops of solid walnut are to-day extremely scarce*, especially examples which would be large enough to be used as dining tables. It may be argued that what has been said about the destruction of walnut bookcases, on page 20, will apply equally to walnut tables, the more so when it is noted in the catalogue of the Chandos sale that there is listed " a walnut-tree dining table." But the reasons put forward to show how walnut bookcases came to be destroyed are not relevant to dining tables. It seems, therefore, a permissible conclusion that, with the introduction of mahogany, the cabinet-makers at once realised that, as it could be obtained in wide planks, it solved the difficulty of making the dining table. They, therefore, swiftly adopted its use in the making of such tables, and this would account for the fact that the earliest pieces of mahogany furniture that are extant are tables†, and that more of them have survived dating prior to 1760 than any other mahogany piece.

A type of mahogany dining table that has survived in considerable numbers has either round straight, or plain cabriole legs ending in club feet, with an oval top similar to the example illustrated, fig. 126. The earliest examples, judging from the design of their legs, appear to date from towards the end of Queen Anne's reign, fig. 125. From this period right up to the last quarter of the eighteenth century, this type of oval flapped table must have been made in very large quantities, as many thousands have survived. They were made in all sizes, from the smallest, sufficient only for two people, to the largest, capable of seating from ten to twelve.

The tripod tea table, similar to examples illustrated, figs. 152 and 154, was another very popular type of table that owed its origin to the introduction of mahogany. These tables had circular or square tops which, from the point of view of appearance, necessitated their being composed of one piece of wood, made possible by the use of mahogany. A tripod table is but seldom found in walnut. This again points to the fact that the cabinet-makers were unable to obtain walnut wood of sufficient width for the top.

In spite of all the advantages possessed by mahogany, it was only used at first very sparsely by the cabinet-makers, as it was an expensive material until the duty on imported timber was removed in 1733. This resulted in a fall in the cost, followed by a greater use of the wood for furniture making.

Mahogany furniture belonging to the first half of the eighteenth century can be divided into two kinds. The first variety is of the highest quality, and is typical of what would have come from the large mansions of the nobility and the rich. Judging from

---

* A number of seventeenth century gate-legged tables are extant with the underframing of walnut and the top of oak or elm.

† A few gate-legged tables of mahogany have survived with turned legs, each leaf of the top formed of one plank. From their design these tables would appear to date from about 1690-1700.

Fig. 125.—Mahogany flap table with oval top.   CIRCA 1715
Fig. 126.—Mahogany flap table with oval top.   CIRCA 1730.

140

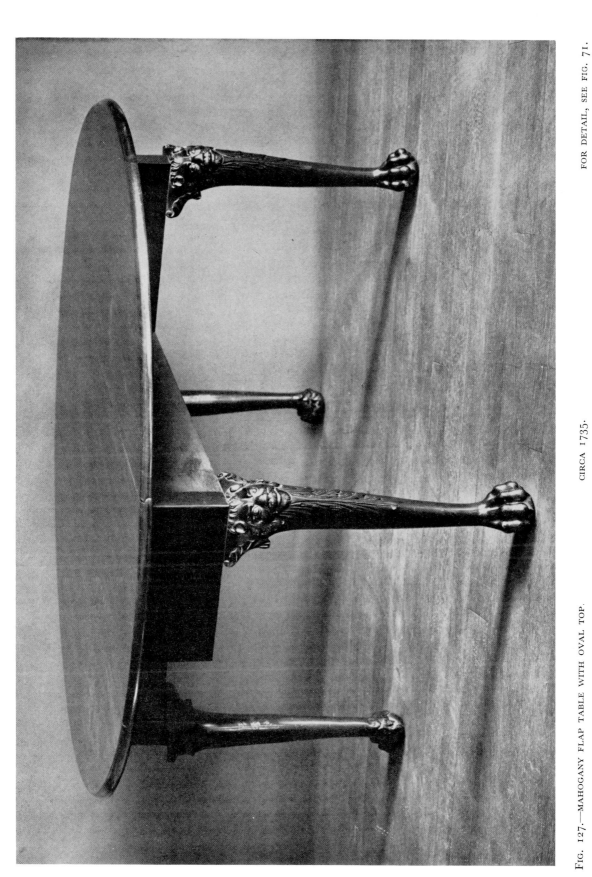

FIG. 127.—MAHOGANY FLAP TABLE WITH OVAL TOP.

CIRCA 1735.

FOR DETAIL, SEE FIG. 71.

141

those pieces that are extant, they are usually side-tables with marble tops, cabinets, library winged bookcases, large library writing tables, fine bureau bookcases, chairs, stools and settees, dining tables, tripod tea tables and card tables.

This fine quality furniture was made in the solid mahogany and not veneered*, and was ornamented with carving. As has already been noted, ornament in the form of carving was the means of relieving the austerity of such pieces, as there was but little figure in the wood.

The second variety of mahogany furniture belonging to this period was of a lower grade of quality. This category includes dining tables and tripod tea tables, which, as already ex-

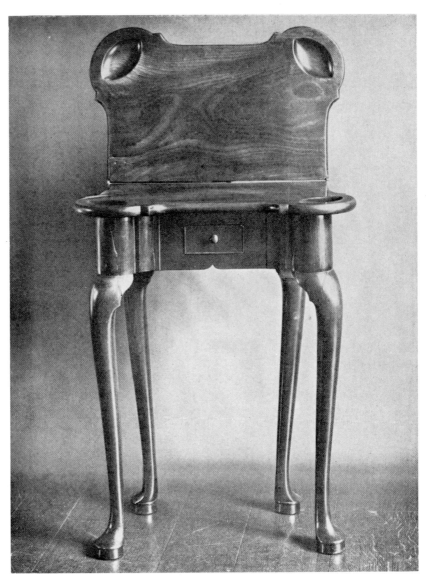

FIG. 128.—SMALL MAHOGANY CARD TABLE, 22 INCHES IN WIDTH.   CIRCA 1740.

plained, were difficult to make in walnut owing to the limitations of that wood.

Besides these two pieces, there are many others which will be found made of mahogany, but, unlike the dining and tea table, they are pieces which were also made in veneered walnut. It is not, therefore, the question of the width of the mahogany plank that caused the cabinet-makers to fashion these examples in mahogany, but because they could be made in the solid wood, which undoubtedly showed a saving in cost as compared with the veneered walnut example. Nearly every type of piece is found in this lower-grade

* Exceptions to this were the seat rails of chairs and friezes of card and side-tables, which were often veneered. The shaped and curved splats of mahogany chairs, similar to the example illustrated, fig. 135, were also veneered, as the continuity of the grain would have been lost if such shaped surfaces had been made of the solid wood. A small number of mahogany pieces are extant which date from about 1725-40, which have all their surfaces veneered in exactly the same manner as a walnut piece of furniture. The construction of a piece in this way may have been in order to economise in the mahogany, in which case it is all the more remarkable, as, in these early veneered examples, the wood is of a plain character, and has but little figure.

quality, but perhaps those that have survived in the greatest number are the card table with cabriole legs ending in club feet, fig. 128, the pedestal dressing table, and the dressing table on round legs terminating in club feet, the toilet mirror and the bachelor chest with folding top, similar in design to the walnut example, fig. 115, bookcases, chairs and stools.

This second-grade mahogany furniture was usually of a plain and austere character, made of dark Spanish mahogany, and undecorated with carving. When carved ornament was employed it was usually confined to the decorating of the knees of the cabriole legs with a small *motif* such as a shell and sometimes a leaf. This type of furniture would appear to date from about 1730-50.

The reason why such furniture could be produced at a lower cost than walnut, even in a period when labour was extremely cheap, is due mainly to the piece being made out of the solid mahogany*, which must have meant a considerable saving in cost when compared with the veneered walnut examples with their tops and drawer fronts decorated with herring-bone inlay and cross-banded edging. Making the mouldings out of the solid wood was also a much easier and cheaper method than constructing them of cross-grained walnut.

Besides the plain mahogany furniture, the cabinet-makers also constructed pieces of a similar character from Virginia walnut. Such furniture, like the mahogany examples, was made out of the solid wood, and the mouldings were also worked in the solid and not cross-grained. A great deal of this furniture, made of Virginia walnut, which dates from about 1720-60, is mistaken to-day for mahogany, as the wood has but little figure and is of a dark colour. Perhaps originally it was stained and polished a dark red colour to make it resemble mahogany furniture. One difference is that the wood bleaches by the action of the sun's rays to a grey tone, while the Spanish mahogany is not affected in this manner (see page 173). Pieces usually found to-day made of Virginia walnut are stools and chairs of the hoop-backed design, and the pedestal dressing table and the example with cabriole legs; also toilet mirrors and tripod pole screens. Many other pieces were undoubtedly made of Virginia walnut; the dining table, however, was an exception, as this American walnut, although planks of it could be obtained in greater width than the English walnut, was not imported in planks of the same width as mahogany. This statement is based on pieces extant, such as the dressing table which, when made from Virginia walnut, usually has the top composed of two planks jointed together.

It would appear, therefore, that mahogany was used in the solid by the cabinet-makers from 1730 to 1745-50 for their finest and most expensive pieces, and, in order to relieve the plainness and severity of the unfigured wood, they used carving as a means of decoration. They also made lower-grade furniture in the solid of mahogany and of Virginia walnut, which, by the omission of carving and veneering, they were able to produce at a lower cost than the contemporary veneered walnut. When they obtained a supply of finely figured mahogany by the importation of the Honduras variety, about 1750-55, they then made mahogany furniture veneered in the manner they had previously made walnut, and, undoubtedly, this was the cause of the cessation of the manufacture of walnut furniture.

* See footnote, page 142

The above review of mahogany furniture up to 1760 is intended to convey a general idea of the first half of the mahogany period. This review has been based upon a consideration of the mahogany pieces that have survived, which offer far more dependable information on the subject than is the case with walnut furniture, because, as already stated, so much of the latter has been destroyed that the amount now extant is an unreliable guide to what was originally made. This is not the case as regards mahogany furniture, however, as the ravages of time have not taken toll of it in the same way, since it was a far stronger and more enduring wood.

In this period the names of the designers and makers of furniture are given for the first time. These names have been handed down, in some cases through the books which were published by cabinet-makers showing the designs for their furniture.

FIG. 129.—MAHOGANY LIBRARY TABLE WITH FOLD-OVER TOP, WITH BASE COMPOSED OF A CHEST-WITH-DRAWERS. THE LION-HEADED TERMINALS PULL OUT TO SUPPORT THE HINGED LEAF.   CIRCA 1740.

THIS PIECE IS STRONGLY REMINISCENT IN DESIGN OF THE KENT SCHOOL OF FURNITURE.

FIG. 130.—DETAIL OF CORNICE OF MAHOGANY BUREAU BOOKCASE, FIG. 131.
THE UNUSUAL KEY DENTIL IS A SIGN OF THE HIGHEST QUALITY.

The first name mentioned in this period, however, is not that of a cabinet-maker, but of an architect, William Kent (1684-1748). Kent was regarded by wealthy and fashionable society, from about 1725 to his death, as an artist of considerable taste, and was much consulted in the decoration and furnishing of houses. In this way he designed a considerable amount of furniture, all of which was ponderous and of a strictly architectural character.

He thought only of the design, and forgot the material in which the design was to be carried out. In consequence, his cabinets and bookcases, although of good architectural proportion and academically correct as regards detail, appear too heavy and massive. An architectural design that is appropriate in brick or stone cannot be satisfactory from an æsthetic point of view if produced in wood. While it is quite possible for furniture to be based on architectural principles, it is essential for the design to be in consonance with the material in which it is being carried out. The design of furniture, therefore, must be sensible to the special limitations and properties of wood.

Furniture designed by a cabinet-maker never erred in this respect. The design might be bad ; but it was invariably a design in harmony with a wood construction. On the other hand, an architect such as Kent disregarded his material, and his design was accurately reproduced in wood by a cabinet-maker who, although working in a material with which he was in complete harmony, did not permit his own individuality to deflect or influence his execution as he meticulously followed Kent's full-size drawings.

This statement is not offered as an historical record of how Kent and his cabinet-makers went to work ; but the bookcases and cabinets which are known to-day to belong to the Kent school of design are æsthetically bad, because of their transgression against the fast principle that the design should be in harmony with the material in which it is to be executed.

Kent's chairs were usually based on the design of contemporary Italian chairs, and therefore show but little originality. In a book published on Kent's work by John Vardy, the design of a chair is given with the front legs in the form of an architectural truss. No designer with any sense of harmony of form would have sanctioned the use of a truss in this manner. It is the effort of a designer who, to achieve originality, sacrifices elegance

FIG. 131.—MAHOGANY BUREAU BOOKCASE OF ARCHITECTURAL DESIGN.   CIRCA 1740.
FOR DETAILS, SEE FIGS. 130 AND 132.

146

of form, which, in design, should be the ultimate object of attainment. Furniture such as Kent's was not traditional. It was a departure from tradition, and fortunately had very little effect on the evolution of the design of English furniture in the eighteenth century.

While Kent was designing his ponderous entablatured bookcases and his pseudo-Italian chairs, the English cabinet-maker was developing his hooped-back chairs with claw-and-ball feet along lighter and more elegant lines, allowing the borrowed French *motif* of a scroll foot to supersede the claw and ball as a termination to the cabriole leg (fig. 161). He borrowed for his bookcases and bureau bookcases architectural features for their adornment, such as Ionic and Corinthian pilasters and entablatures, often surmounted by broken pediments (fig. 131). This furniture definitely took its place in the evolution of eighteenth century furniture design. It did not transgress any principle, as the workmen who made it, and the cabinet-maker who designed it, had each the same knowledge of and feeling for their common craft, in which they had worked since the days of their apprenticeship. It is when furniture is designed by someone who has not an intimate knowledge of the craft of furniture-making that the design is deficient, since the same common understanding cannot exist between designer and craftsman.

A phase of design between the years 1725 and 1745, peculiar to mahogany furniture, was the fashion for decorating the legs of chairs and tables with masks, and the arms of chairs with bird and animal heads. Mention of this, as regards walnut furniture, has been made on page 25, and the same remarks are equally applicable to mahogany furniture.

FIG. 132.—DETAIL SHOWING DRAWERS AND PIGEON-HOLES OF MAHOGANY BUREAU BOOKCASE, FIG. 131.

FIG. 133.—MAHOGANY ARMCHAIR WITH ARMS TERMINATING IN LIONS' HEADS. CIRCA 1730.

The next name that occurs in the history of the evolution of English furniture is that of a cabinet - maker named Thomas Chippendale. That his name to-day is a household word is due to his having published a book of his designs entitled *The Gentleman and Cabinet Maker's Director.* The first edition appeared in 1754, and subsequent editions in 1759 and 1762. Unquestionably, Thomas Chippendale was a cabinet-maker in a large way of business with a fashionable and wealthy *clientèle.* He made furniture of the highest quality, and the fact that he published a book certainly helped to disseminate his designs among provincial cabinet - makers. These designs show furniture in the French, Chinese and Gothic styles, and, within recent years, these styles have been ascribed to him as their creator. But there is abundant evidence to disprove this absurd statement. The French, Chinese and Gothic styles of ornament that were introduced into furniture about the middle of the eighteenth century appeared first of all in the interior decoration of houses, and were used in connection with chimney-pieces, staircases and other interior fitments made by the joiner. Chinese design was also much in vogue for garden furniture, bridges and pavilions. The design of joiners' work for interior fitments of houses was always ten or fifteen years earlier than that of the cabinet-maker's. When Chippendale was making the designs for his book he was naturally working in these three styles, which were the common property of all cabinet-makers conforming to the then latest fashions, and he was not therefore evolving anything new. Other contemporary cabinet-makers also published books illustrating furniture of almost identical design; in fact, so nearly

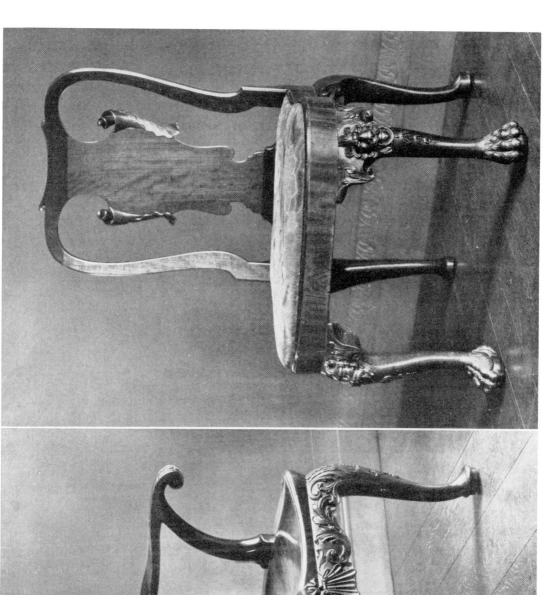

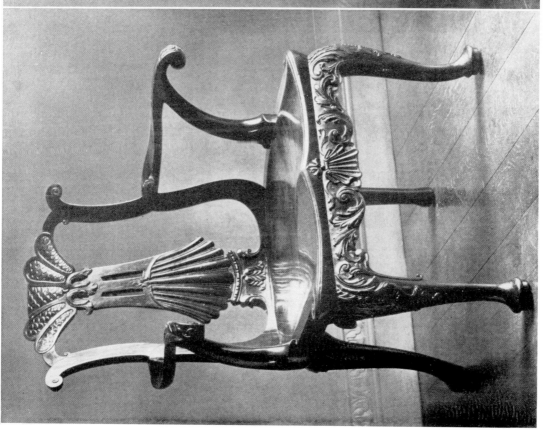

FIG. 134.—MAHOGANY ARMCHAIR.

CIRCA 1735.

FIG. 135.—MAHOGANY CHAIR WITH VENEERED SPLAT ON MAHOGANY FOUNDATION.
CIRCA 1730.

FOR DETAIL, SEE FIG. 69.

149

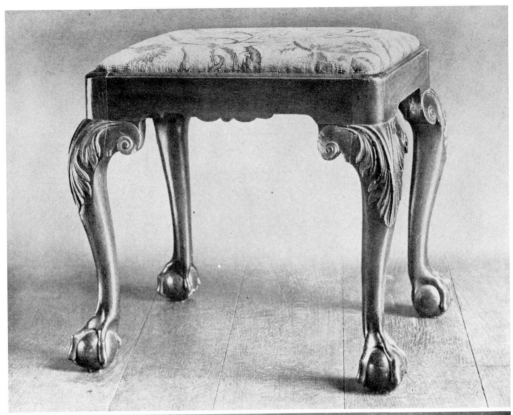

FIG. 136.—WALNUT STOOL. CIRCA 1740.

FIG. 137.—MAHOGANY STOOL BELONGING TO THE SET OF CHAIRS ILLUSTRATED IN FIGS. 172 AND 173.

CIRCA 1755.

related are the designs in Chippendale's book to those of his contemporaries, that it would be impossible to decide definitely on their individual origin. Chippendale's are perhaps a little more elaborate, but, from an artistic point of view, they gain nothing thereby. Of the cabinet-makers who published books of designs about the same time as Chippendale, the following can be named : Ince and Mayhew, A Society of Upholsterers and Cabinet Makers, Robert Manwaring, and Mathias Lock. Although these publications were all later than the first edition of the *Director*, it is extremely unlikely that the authors were in every case copying Chippendale's designs. They were all, including Chippendale, merely showing their designs for furniture in the current taste of the period.

As Thomas Chippendale was not the originator of the French, Chinese and Gothic styles in furniture, no piece in any of these styles can rightly be termed Chippendale, unless his actual invoice has survived with it.

There is also no justification for using his name in the generic sense, which would only be permissible if a style could be definitely attributed to him.

It has also been asserted that pieces which can be proved by documentary evidence to have come from his workshop are unique in the very high standard of their technical excellence. The mahogany furniture of the period of 1730-40, at which time Chippendale was a young man still in his twenties, is of the same high quality as regards cabinet-making and carving. Surely the unknown cabinet-makers who were responsible for this furniture still continued to make it at the time that Chippendale was producing his. Therefore, there is no justification for declaring a piece, because it is of the highest quality and is of Chippendale's time, to be the product of his workshop.

On the contemporary evidence available it is not possible to admit that in the eighteenth century Chippendale was considered anything more than a successful tradesman, and one specially noteworthy for making furniture of very good quality. To-day, however, his fame has been extolled to such a degree that he holds the position of an original artist of considerable taste, the creator of a style of design, and the arbiter of fashion in furniture. Many people, in fact, deem it correct to describe all mahogany furniture up to the last quarter of the eighteenth century as " Chippendale."

A well-known furniture authority within recent years ascribed to Chippendale, in addition to his other attributes, a craftsmanship of the highest quality. Furthermore, he presumed to be able to say that a certain piece was undoubtedly by the hand of Thomas Chippendale himself, as he was able to recognise Chippendale's individual touch wherever it occurred. There is no evidence to support this assumption that Chippendale was a carver ; and, even if he were, no authenticated piece carved by his own hand has survived to justify this extravagant assertion.

The absurdity of making Chippendale* the one and only outstanding character in the craft of cabinet-making in the mid-eighteenth century will become immediately apparent when this period is viewed in its proper perspective. The demand for furniture

---

* One contemporary reference which goes to show his status is a mention of him in the *Gentleman's Magazine* when his workshop was burnt down. He is there described as " Mr. Chippendale, a cabinet maker, near St Martins lane." From this description it would appear that he was not an important personage, but just one of many cabinet-makers.

N

FIG. 138.—MARBLE SLAB CONSOLE TABLE ON MAHOGANY FRAME.
CIRCA 1745.

must have been considerable, and the craft of furniture-making a very important one throughout the country. There were many thousands of firms, both large and small, all of whom employed more or less skilled craftsmen. These firms were not by any means all situated in London, although there were many important groups of cabinet-makers established there. One of the centres for furniture warehouses was St. Paul's Church Yard ; the trade label of Benjamin Crook (see fig. 139) bears this address.

It must be realised that there were many more important people in the eighteenth century than those few whose names have come down to us. At the time, those names which are now household words were probably quite unimportant and of but little consequence to tens of thousands of eighteenth century householders ; whereas individuals, whose names and fame may have been the talk of the town in their day, are now completely unknown. It is not so easy to visualise the eighteenth century as people imagine, who are content to populate it with a dozen or more celebrities and forget the existence of those whose fame died with them.

The Chinese and Gothic furniture, dating from 1750-70, was a very bad break in the evolution of eighteenth century furniture design. The craze for novelty resulted in the cabinet-makers throwing tradition to the winds. These

FIG. 139.—DETAIL SHOWING TRADE LABEL OF BENJAMIN CROOK
PASTED IN DRAWER OF WALNUT CARD TABLE, FIG. 25.

FIG. 140.—MAHOGANY DRESSING TABLE WITH SERPENTINE FRONT.   CIRCA 1755.   THE FRONTS OF THE DRAWERS AND THE CUPBOARD DOOR ARE VENEERED WITH FINELY FIGURED CUBAN MAHOGANY, AND THE CANTED CORNERS ARE DECORATED WITH FINELY CUT APPLIED FRET (FIG. 142).   THE TOP DRAWER IS FITTED WITH A TOILET MIRROR AND BOXES (FIG. 141).   THIS IS AN EXTREMELY FINE EXAMPLE.

153

new styles were so foreign to the spirit of the old designs that their originators, instead of using their traditional training to design a structure in keeping with the new style, transposed the Chinese and Gothic *motifs* on to the old structure. This applied especially to bookcases and cabinets. Fortunately, however, this Chinese furniture of elaborate design was not often carried out in mahogany, as it was generally made in soft wood and afterwards lacquered or gilt, and has in consequence since perished.

Many pieces, at the same time, have survived from this period which are of excellent design, due to the restrained use of the Chinese and Gothic *motifs* and a refusal to allow

FIG. 141.—DETAIL OF THE FITTED DRAWER OF MAHOGANY DRESSING TABLE, FIG. 140.

them to predominate over the structure of the piece. Chinese and Gothic ornament, when used in the form of a fret to decorate the frieze of a cornice or the gallery of a table (figs. 140, 151 and 207-8), is a pleasant variation, as, in such a position, it is subordinate to the structure and therefore permissible on a piece which is neither Gothic nor Chinese in form.

A design that was introduced from about 1735-40, and which is more typical of mahogany furniture than walnut, was that known as the serpentine front. This design was applied to card tables, commodes, chests-with-drawers, wardrobes, side-tables, sideboards and a number of other articles, also pieces of small dimensions, such as pot cupboards, centre tea tables and urn stands ; the last two, however, had the serpentine shape on all four sides. The exact date when it originated is difficult to determine, but certainly one of the earliest pieces known with this serpentine shape is the walnut card table illustrated, fig. 34. After 1750 it became a very popular feature of design, and

FIG. 142.—DETAIL SHOWING APPLIED FRET
ORNAMENT ON CANTED CORNER OF MAHOGANY
DRESSING TABLE, FIG. 140.

FIG. 143.—DETAIL OF APPLIED FRET ORNAMENT
ON CANTED CORNER OF WARDROBE, FIG. 144.

continued in favour up to the end of the eighteenth century, when designers such as
Hepplewhite and Sheraton made extensive use of it in their furniture.

MATERIAL.

The first variety of mahogany that was imported for the making of furniture was
known as Spanish or San Domingo mahogany. This came from the West Indies and
was termed Spanish, because of the then Spanish dominion over those Islands. As already
mentioned, this type of mahogany was a heavy, hard and close-grained timber. The
early mahogany furniture made from it, which includes that of the William Kent school
of design, had little figure or marking in the wood. This lack of figure, however, is not
typical of Spanish mahogany, since it is a wood which often exhibits the finest figuring.
About the middle of the eighteenth century, a different variety of mahogany, known as

FIG. 144.—MAHOGANY WARDROBE WITH SERPENTINE FRONT.   CIRCA 1760.   THIS EXAMPLE IS OF THE FINEST
QUALITY CRAFTSMANSHIP AND IS VERY SIMILAR IN DESIGN TO WARDROBES ILLUSTRATED IN CHIPPENDALE'S *Director*.

Cuban, was imported, which was less heavy than the Spanish, but was also of a hard, close texture. It was noteworthy for a special marking, known as " curls," which was obtained by cutting the wood through the fork of the main tree where it is joined by a large branch. Twin trees, which have grown together, will also give the wood a similar figuring. Sheraton, in his *Cabinet Dictionary*, mentions Cuban mahogany :—

" the island of Cuba is a Spanish colony, and was first discovered by Columbus, a Spanish navigator, in 1492. That, however, which is generally distinguished by Spanish mahogany is finer than what is called Cuba, which is pale, straight grained, and some of it only a bastard kind of mahogany.

" It is generally used for chair wood, for which some of it will do very well."

One important difference between the Spanish and the Cuban mahogany is that the former grows darker with age, until it is nearly black in tone, whereas the latter remains a light colour and mellows only to a rich brown tint.

A third kind of mahogany, known as Honduras, was used extensively by the cabinet-makers in the last half of the eighteenth century. This wood is much lighter in weight and softer in texture than either the Spanish or the Cuban. The following reference to this wood by Sheraton is of considerable interest. He writes :—

" From this province [Honduras] is imported the principal kind of mahogany in use amongst cabinet-makers, which generally bears the name of Honduras mahogany, and sometimes Bay-wood, from the bay or arm of the sea which runs up to it. The difference between Honduras and Spanish wood is easily perceived by judges, but not by others unskilled in wood. The marks of the former are, as to size, its length and width, which generally run much more than in the latter wood. We seldom import any much more than 2 feet 2 inches broad and 10 feet long, and generally not more than 21 or 22 inches broad. Honduras wood will frequently run 12 to 14 feet in length, and from 2 to 4 feet wide. In rare instances, there have been some 6 or 7 feet over.

" The grain of Honduras wood is of a different quality from that of Cuba, which is close and hard, without black speckles, and of a rosy hue, and sometimes strongly figured ; but Honduras wood is of an open nature, with black or grey spots, and frequently of a more flashy figure than Spanish. The best quality of Honduras wood is known by its being free from chalky and black speckles, and when the colour is inclined to a dark gold hue. The common sort of it looks brisk at a distance, and of a lively pale red ; but, on close inspection, is of an open and close grain, and of a spongy appearance."

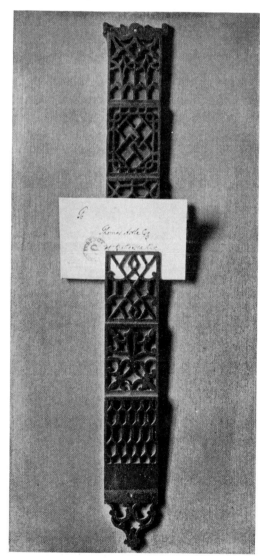

FIG. 145.—MAHOGANY LETTER RACK.   CIRCA 1770.

There were varying degrees of quality as regards the figure and the marking of the wood in all three varieties of mahogany.

The Honduras variety was undoubtedly an inferior one when compared with Spanish and Cuban. It was used in the solid for the sides of pieces and for drawer fronts and linings. The wood that had a fine figure was used extensively for veneering in the last half of the eighteenth century, as has already been mentioned.

When a set of chairs is found of soft Honduras mahogany, it indicates that this wood has been used for reasons of economy, and that the chairs are of a lower grade than if made of Cuban mahogany.

A chair made of Honduras mahogany is much lighter in weight than one of Cuban. The former will seldom exhibit any figuring in the wood, whereas a chair of Cuban mahogany will sometimes show definite marking. Such a feature is generally associated with a good quality chair.

CONSTRUCTION AND WORKMANSHIP.

Mahogany furniture up to about 1750 was generally made in the solid wood and

not veneered; that is, with the exceptions already mentioned on page 142. The cabinet-makers did not use the figure and grain of the wood as a form of decoration; this early school of mahogany furniture, with its dark, sometimes almost black tone, being in consequence of a severe and plain character, save when in the best quality pieces it was relieved with carving

The remarks made previously with regard to dovetails*, drawer linings†, and dust-boards of the walnut furniture of the last quarter of the walnut period apply equally to mahogany. Rounded edges to the top of the drawer sides will be seldom found on pieces of mahogany furniture later than 1750, as after this date the cabinet-makers made

FIG. 146.—DETAIL SHOWING SATYR MASK ON KNEE AND CLOVEN-HOOFED FOOT OF LEG OF MAHOGANY TRIPOD TABLE, FIG. 187.

* About 1780, which is outside the period of this book, drawer bottoms were fixed to the sides by a grooved fillet (see diagram 2d). Such a construction can always be recognised by the presence of these fillets which can be seen inside the drawer, fitted against the drawer sides, and should be remembered, as no drawer with its bottom fixed in this manner can be earlier than 1775-80.

† Mahogany furniture of good quality dating from 1770 often had the drawer linings of mahogany. Cedar was also used for the drawer linings of pieces of bedroom furniture, and sometimes for the small drawers of bureaux. The use of cedar for this purpose is a sign of quality, as it would add to the cost of the piece.

FIG. 147.—DETAIL OF THE LION MASK ON THE LEG OF
THE MAHOGANY TABLE, FIG. 177.

FIG. 148.—DETAIL SHOWING LION MASK MOTIF ON LEG
OF MAHOGANY CHAIR, FIG. 168.

these edges square. When veneered mahogany furniture began to be made about 1750, only the front of a piece was veneered with fine figured wood, the sides being made of solid and plain mahogany. The fronts of veneered drawers in good quality pieces were made in mahogany, and in poorer quality pieces, of deal. Oak was also employed in good quality pieces, but

FIG. 149.—DETAIL OF LEG OF MAHOGANY BUREAU
BOOKCASE, FIG. 210.

in a lesser degree than mahogany. The backs of pieces dating from 1750-60 were panelled, and not made out of boards as hitherto. This practice started about the middle of the eighteenth century. Usually these backs were of deal, but those of fine pieces were of oak. The front of a serpentine or shaped drawer would have the carcase wood constructed in two or three layers, and not in one solid piece.   This was done to prevent the drawer front twisting.   Sometimes, when the foundation of the drawer front was mahogany, it was made in one piece. Large mouldings, such as those of a cornice to a bookcase, were built up with strips of mahogany which were backed on to a deal foundation (diagram 5d).

The quality of the workmanship of the first grade of mahogany furniture was exceptionally high ; in fact, it can be termed superlative, whilst that of the lower grade also exhibited good craftsmanship, as it was not until 1760 that the cabinet-makers began to make mahogany furniture of inferior workmanship.   This good craftsmanship of the lower-grade furniture, however, only applies to the actual cabinet work and not to the carving, as when carving does occur it is sometimes found of a very coarse character.   In the first grade, however, the carving is of the highest quality, especially the architectural pieces of the Kent school of design, and also that on chairs, especially those dating from 1740-60.   This question of the quality of the carving is of considerable importance, and recognition of its various grades is essential.

FIG. 150.—DETAIL OF GROTESQUE MASK ON LEG OF MAHOGANY TRIPOD TABLE, FIG. 183.

In fine quality work the acanthus foliage was in high relief, and the scroll of the foliage intertwined, revealing the most delicate rendering of the smallest detail.   Poor quality carved acanthus foliage was shallow, and generally exhibited a number of gouged lines on the surface, showing none of the intertwining of the tendrils so typical of fine quality carving.

Careful examination of the backs of many chairs will show that there are different grades of quality in the carving from superb to mediocre and coarse.   The highest quality will be seldom found, but when it is, it should be quickly recognised, as this quality determines the intrinsic value of a piece far more than any pedigree denoting that it came from Chippendale's workshop.   It is design and quality which count, and not pedigrees. A pedigree may have historic interest, but it cannot endow a piece with an artistic merit which it does not possess.

The illustrations depicting details of furniture, figs. 147, 148, 150, and 164, show examples of the highest quality carving in mahogany.   The rendering of the cabriole leg

Fig. 151.—MAHOGANY TEA TABLE WITH GALLERY OF PIERCED FRET.   CIRCA 1755.   THE ELEGANT AND GRACEFUL CURVE OF THE LEGS IS A NOTEWORTHY FEATURE OF THIS TABLE.   THE TOP IS OF MAHOGANY OF AN UNUSUAL FIGURE, KNOWN AS "BLISTER."

FIG. 152.—MAHOGANY TRIPOD TABLE WITH GALLERY TOP. CIRCA 1750. FIG. 153.—DETAIL OF TOP SHOWING GALLERY. THIS TABLE IS ONE OF A PAIR.

FIG. 154.—MAHOGANY TRIPOD TABLE.   CIRCA 1745.

FIG. 155.—DETAIL OF TOP, MEASUREMENT 32¼ INCHES DIAMETER.

163

Fig. 156.—MAHOGANY CARD TABLE WITH PROJECTING CORNERS TO TOP TO ACCOMMODATE CANDLESTICKS.
CIRCA 1755.

Fig. 157.—MAHOGANY CARD TABLE.   CIRCA 1755.

164

is an important sign of quality as regards chairs and tables. In a well-designed leg the cabriole has a graceful curve, and terminates in a claw foot that will have the appearance, not only of firmly gripping the ball, but of being set at such a well-poised angle that it actually contributes to the strength of the leg, and thus to the support of the seat or table. The leg and foot will be in consonance with each other, which will result in giving a feeling of unity to the whole design.

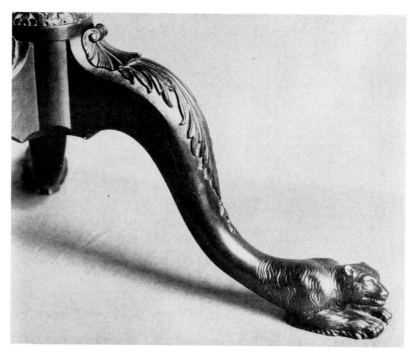

FIG. 158.—DETAIL OF LEG OF MAHOGANY FIRE SCREEN ILLUSTRATED, FIG. 200.

In a badly rendered cabriole leg the graceful curve will be absent, and the foot will appear to be clumsily attached and not in harmony with the leg. Such a leg is often too heavy at the knee and too thin in the middle, or *vice versa*. As examples of well-executed cabriole legs the illustrations, figs. 151, 156, 157, 169 and 170, should be examined.

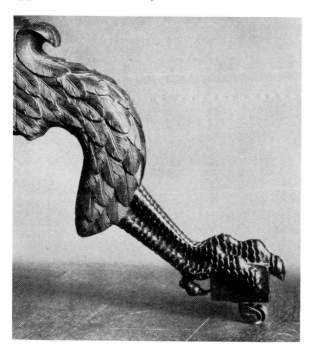

FIG. 159.—DETAIL OF LEG OF MAHOGANY DUMB-WAITER, FIG. 202.

O

METHODS OF POLISHING.

Exactly what methods were employed for polishing mahogany furniture belonging to the first half of the eighteenth century is a matter of surmise. It was certainly done with oil, and, since mahogany was a hard wood and could be polished by friction, it must have been an easier process than the varnishing and subsequent polishing of walnut wood, as already described.

It is necessary to apply to Thomas Sheraton for the recipes for polishing mahogany furniture, since in his *Cabinet*

Dictionary, published in 1803, he makes mention of the various methods of polishing used by the cabinet-makers in the latter half of the eighteenth century. Whether they used other methods, than those Sheraton mentions, in the early part of the mahogany period it is difficult to say.

In the mahogany period under review, from examples extant, it would appear that

mahogany furniture was not varnished with the shellac varnish and then polished. Later eighteenth century pieces, especially fine quality satinwood examples, were undoubtedly sometimes polished in this manner, as a number have survived with a surface of highly polished varnish.

A recipe for polishing mahogany with oil is here given from Sheraton's *Dictionary*. He writes :—

" The root [of Akanet] is much in use amongst cabinet-makers, for making red oil ; the best composition for which, as far as I know, is as follows : take a quart of good linseed oil, to which put a quarter of a pound of akanet root, as much opened with the hand as possible, that the bark of the root which tinges the oil may fly off ; to this put about an ounce of dragon's blood, and another of rose pink, finely pounded in a mortar ; set the whole within a moderate heat for twelve hours at least,

FIG. 160.—DETAIL OF CARVED SPLAT OF MAHOGANY CHAIR, FIGS. 161 AND 162.

or better if a day and a night. Then strain it through a flannel into a bottle for use. This staining oil is not properly applicable to every sort of mahogany. The open grained honduras ought first to be polished with wax and turpentine to fill up the grain ; but in general this wood looks best with wax and turpentine only ; but if it be tolerably close-grained and hard and wants briskness of colour, the above oil will help it much. All hard mahogany of a bad colour should be oiled with it, and should stand unpolished a time, proportioned to its quality and texture of grain ; if it be laid on hard wood to be polished off immediately, it is of little use ; but if it stand a few days after, the oil penetrates the grain and hardens on the surface, and consequently will bear a better polish, and look brighter in colour."

Fig. 161.—MAHOGANY ARMCHAIR, SHOWING STRONG FRENCH INFLUENCE IN ITS DESIGN.   CIRCA 1760.
FOR BACK VIEW AND DETAIL OF SPLAT, SEE FIGS. 162 AND 160.

167

Fig. 162.—Back view of chair illustrated Fig. 161.

In the eighteenth century the colour most sought after for mahogany was red, and unquestionably many of those pieces that to-day have a nut-brown colour were originally of a reddish tone. Age and exposure to the atmosphere have caused the reddish tone

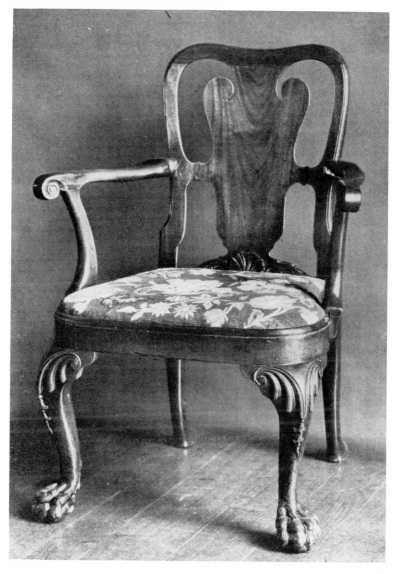

FIG. 163.—MAHOGANY ARMCHAIR WITH SPLAT OF SOLID WOOD.   C. 1735.
FOR DETAIL, SEE FIG. 167.

of the wood to mellow to a brown. The foregoing quotation mentions polishing with wax and turpentine. Another method of polishing with wax is also described by Sheraton, when he says :—

"Chairs are generally polished with a hardish composition of wax rubbed upon a polishing brush, with which the grain of the wood is impregnated with the composition, and afterward well rubbed off."

FIG. 164.—DETAIL SHOWING CRESTING OF MAHOGANY CHAIR, FIG. 165.

In *The Cabinet-Makers' London Book of Prices*, published in 1803, mention is also made of wax and oil polishing to the effect that :—

" Polishing the outside of any work with hard wax to be double the price of oil polishing.

" Ditto with turpentine and wax to be half the price extra from oil polishing."

The above quotations are definite proof that there were three methods of polishing in the late eighteenth century ; but whether these were practised in the earlier part of the century it is not possible to say. Undoubtedly, chairs were polished with hard wax and also with oil.

Sheraton gives a very full description of how oil polishing was carried out. He writes :—

" The general mode of polishing plain cabinet work is however with oil and brick-dust."

And again :—

" If the wood be hard, the oil should be left standing upon it for a week ; but if soft, it may be polished in two days. The brick-dust and oil should then be rubbed together, which in a little time will become a putty under the rubbing cloth, in which state it should be kept under the cloth as much as possible ; for this kind of putty will infallibly secure a fine polish by continued rubbing ; and the polisher should by all means avoid the application of fresh brick-dust, by which the unskilful hand will frequently ruin his work instead of improving it : and to prevent the necessity of supplying himself with fresh brick-dust he ought to lay on a great quantity at first, carefully sifted through a gauze stocking ; and he should notice if the oil be too dry on the surface of the work before he begin, for in this case it should be re-oiled, that it may compose a sufficient quantity of the polishing substance, which should never be altered after the polishing is commenced, and which ought to continue till the wood by repeated friction become warm, at which time it will finish in a bright polish, and is finally to be cleared off with the bran of wheaten flour."

FIG. 165.—MASONIC MASTER'S MAHOGANY CHAIR.   CIRCA 1740.   FOR DETAIL, SEE FIG. 164

171

This method of polishing could not have been carried out on carved work very satisfactorily, and was accordingly confined to table tops and plain cabinet work, as Sheraton suggests.

FIG. 166.—MAHOGANY ARMCHAIR.   CIRCA 1770.
THE DESIGN OF THE ARMS OF THIS CHAIR IS PARTICULARLY GOOD.

Undoubtedly, the effect of oil on mahogany was to darken the wood. It would appear correct, therefore, to surmise that those pieces which are dark in tone, such as the early mahogany furniture, were polished with oil. Polishing with wax would have resulted in the wood remaining a more natural colour, much lighter in tone. The softer Honduras mahogany, as Sheraton says, did not polish so well with oil, since the spongy nature of the wood absorbed it, making the mahogany in consequence too dark.

One fact about mahogany furniture is that the polish, as found on the piece with its original surface, has been greatly improved by the domestic polishing that the piece has received since it was made. Cornices of bookcases which, owing to their position, are not accessible to the duster, exhibit a dryness and an unpolished surface. The unexposed parts of carving in high relief also have the same unpolished appearance. This especially applies to the mahogany furniture of the first half of the eighteenth century. The carving and mouldings of such a piece when originally polished must have looked very dry and untreated owing to the difficulty of polishing those portions with oil or wax. On a flat, plain surface this did not apply.

The effects of exposure to the light and air on Spanish and Cuban mahogany were to darken the wood ; nor were they affected to any considerable extent by sunlight, as they did not easily bleach to a paler colour. Honduras mahogany, on the contrary, was not darkened by exposure to the air, and was bleached to a much lighter colour when exposed to the rays of the sun. Mellowing or bleaching only affected the outer skin, as, if the surface of the mahogany is cleaned off with a solvent or scraped, it will, on repolishing, assume a red colour. This is one of the reasons why the French polishing of old mahogany is so detrimental to its appearance, as it turns the mellow brown colour of age to a reddish tint. It is true that our eighteenth century ancestors admired this reddish colour ; but, to-day, modern taste appreciates the beauty of the nut-brown colour conferred upon the wood by the gradual patination of its surface through time.

Fig. 167.—DETAIL OF CARVED SHOE PIECE OF MAHOGANY CHAIR, FIG. 163.

FIG. 168.—MAHOGANY ARMCHAIR WITH PETIT-POINT NEEDLEWORK COVERING.   CIRCA 1745.
THIS CHAIR IS OF EXCEPTIONALLY FINE PROPORTIONS, AND THE QUALITY OF THE CARVING IS SUPERLATIVE.
FOR DETAILS, SEE FIGS. 20 AND 148.

174

FIG. 169.—MAHOGANY ARMCHAIR.   CIRCA 1745.

THIS CHAIR, WHICH IS OF LARGE DIMENSIONS, IS OF EXCEPTIONALLY FINE PROPORTIONS AND QUALITY.

175

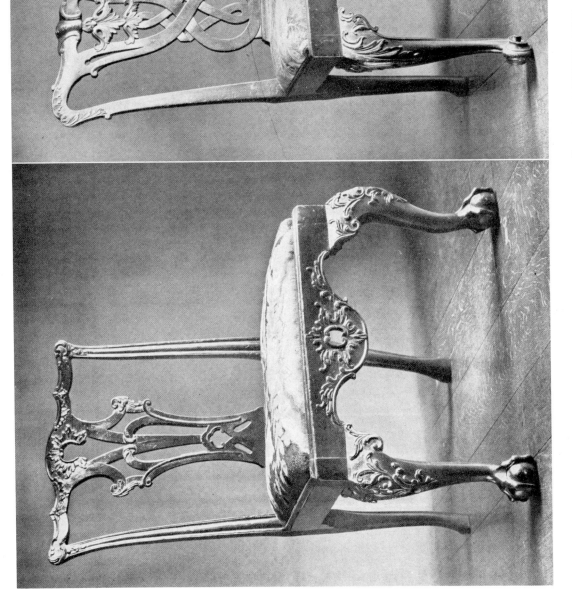

FIG. 170.—MAHOGANY CHAIR WITH UNUSUAL CARVED ORNAMENT TO SEAT RAIL.
CIRCA 1755.

FIG. 171.—MAHOGANY CHAIR.
CIRCA 1760.

ONE OF A PAIR.

P

176

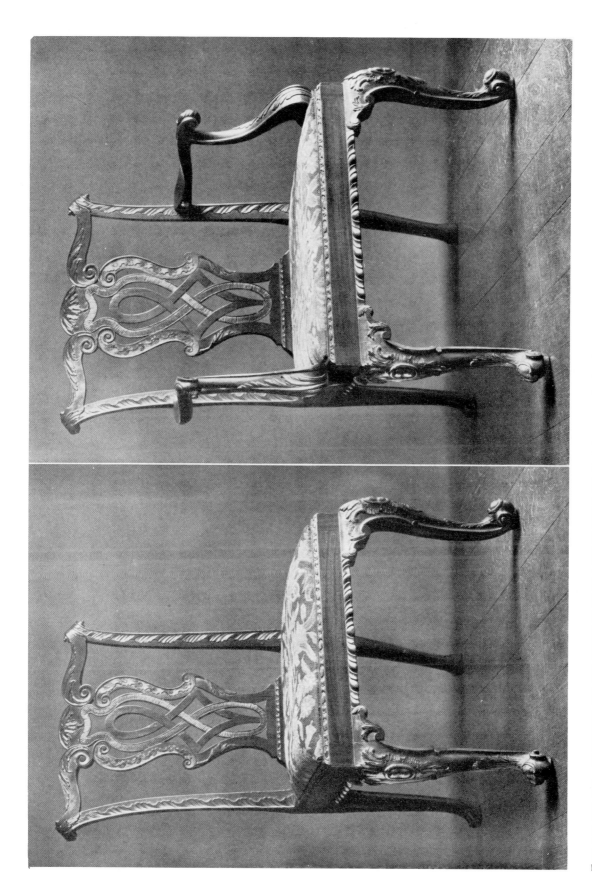

FIGS. 172 AND 173.—MAHOGANY ARM AND SINGLE CHAIR OF A SET OF EIGHT AND TWO ARMS.   CIRCA 1755.   THIS SET IS MADE OF FINE QUALITY CUBAN MAHOGANY.

177

FIGS. 174 AND 175.—TWO MAHOGANY CHAIRS.   CIRCA 1750.   THESE TWO CHAIRS UNDOUBTEDLY ONCE BELONGED TO SETS OF DINING ROOM CHAIRS.
THE SIMILARITY IN THE GENERAL DESIGN OF THE BACKS SHOULD BE NOTED.

178

FIG. 176.—MARBLE SLAB TABLE ON MAHOGANY FRAME.
3 FEET 4 INCHES IN WIDTH.

THE LEAF MOTIF ON THE KNEE OF THE LEG IS UNUSUAL.
CIRCA 1740.

179

FIG. 177.—MARBLE SLAB CONSOLE TABLE ON MAHOGANY FRAME.   3 FEET 9 INCHES IN WIDTH.   CIRCA 1735.
THE BOLD AND SKILFUL EXECUTION OF THE MASKS ON THE LEGS BETRAYS THE HIGHEST QUALITY OF CRAFTSMANSHIP.   FOR DETAIL, SEE FIG. 147.

180

Fig. 178.—Marble slab table on walnut frame.   Circa 1735.   This is an exceptional walnut example.

181

FIG. 179.—MARBLE SLAB TABLE ON MAHOGANY FRAME.

5 FEET 6 INCHES IN WIDTH.   CIRCA 1740.

182

FIG. 180.—MARBLE SLAB TABLE ON MAHOGANY FRAME.   5 FEET 8 INCHES IN WIDTH.   CIRCA 1740.   THIS TABLE IS VERY SIMILAR IN DESIGN TO FIG. 179. THE EXCEPTIONALLY BOLD LEG AND LARGE CLAW AND BALL FOOT MUST HAVE DEMANDED A VERY BIG LOG OF MAHOGANY, AS BOTH THE LEG AND FOOT ARE CARVED OUT OF ONE PIECE.

FIG. 181.—SCAGLIOLA SLAB TABLE ON MAHOGANY FRAME. 3 FEET 2 INCHES IN WIDTH. CIRCA 1755.
THE UNUSUAL FEATURE OF THIS TABLE IS THAT THE FRONT IS SERPENTINE.

184

185

FIG. 182.—MARBLE SLAB TABLE ON MAHOGANY FRAME.   4 FEET 6 INCHES IN WIDTH.   CIRCA 1760.   THE CARVED MASK IN THE MIDDLE OF
THE FRIEZE IS A RARE FEATURE.

FIG. 183.—MAHOGANY TRIPOD TABLE WITH GALLERY TOP, AND KNEES DECORATED WITH MASKS.   CIRCA 1750. THIS TABLE IS OF AN EXCEPTIONALLY WELL PROPORTIONED AND GRACEFUL DESIGN, AND IS OF THE HIGHEST QUALITY WORKMANSHIP.   THE MASKS ARE TYPICAL BOTH AS REGARDS DESIGN AND EXECUTION OF EIGHTEENTH CENTURY CRAFTSMANSHIP.   SEE DETAIL FIG. 150.   ANOTHER UNUSUAL FEATURE OF THIS TABLE IS THE DESIGN OF THE CIRCULAR BIRD-CAGE BY WHICH THE TOP IS FIXED TO THE STEM.

FIGS. 184 AND 185.—MAHOGANY TRIPOD TABLE WITH PIE-CRUST TOP OF UNUSUAL DESIGN DECORATED WITH ACANTHUS FOLIAGE.
THE FINE QUALITY OF THE MAHOGANY FORMING THE TOP SHOULD BE NOTED.

CIRCA 1755.

Q

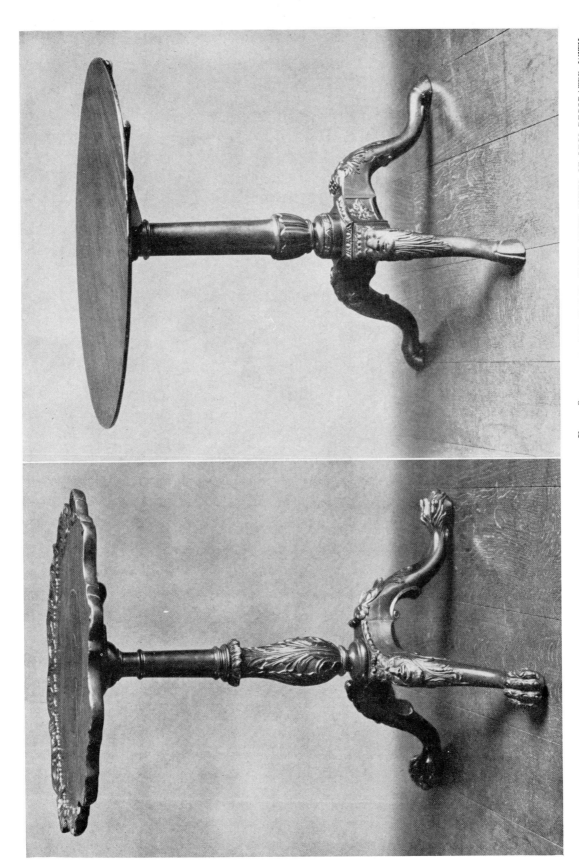

Fig. 186.—Irish mahogany tripod table with knees of legs decorated with satyr mask motif. Circa 1745.

Fig. 187.—Mahogany tripod table with knees of legs decorated with satyr mask motif. Circa 1740. For detail of leg, see Fig. 146.

189

FIGS. 188 AND 189.—MAHOGANY TRIPOD TABLE.　　CIRCA 1755.

THE TOP OF THIS TABLE IS VERY SIMILAR TO THE EXAMPLE, FIG. 185.

FIG. 190.—MAHOGANY TRIPOD TABLE WITH BOLD PAW FEET.   CIRCA 1745.   FIG. 191.—MAHOGANY TRIPOD TABLE.   CIRCA 1755.

190

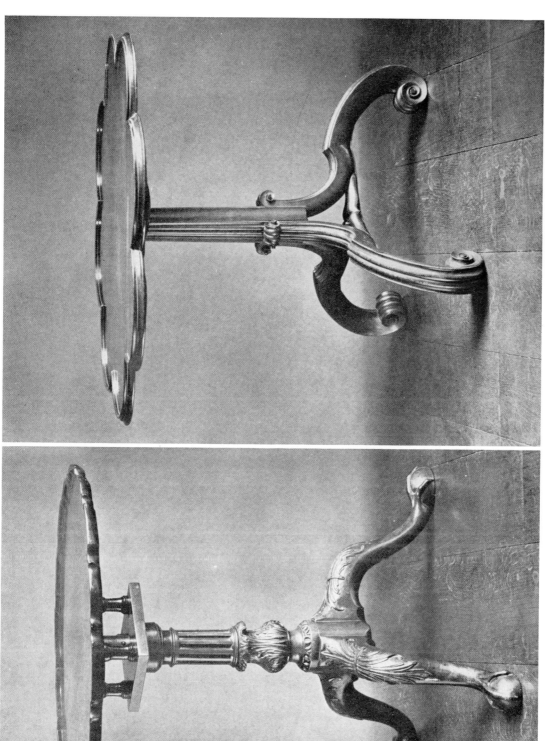

FIG. 192.—MAHOGANY TRIPOD TABLE.　　　CIRCA 1755.　　　FIG. 193.—MAHOGANY TRIPOD TABLE.　　CIRCA 1760.

FIG. 193, ALTHOUGH PLAIN IN CHARACTER, IS OF AN EXCEPTIONALLY GRACEFUL AND WELL PROPORTIONED DESIGN.

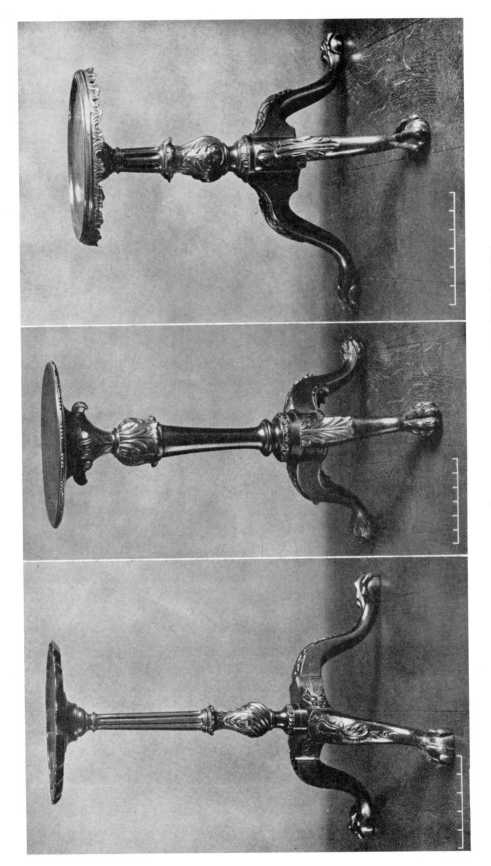

Figs. 194, 195 and 196.—Three mahogany tripod tea-kettle stands.

These stands were for holding a kettle, with spirit lamp, by the side of a tea table.

Figs. 194 and 196 circa 1750, and Fig. 195 circa 1735.

192

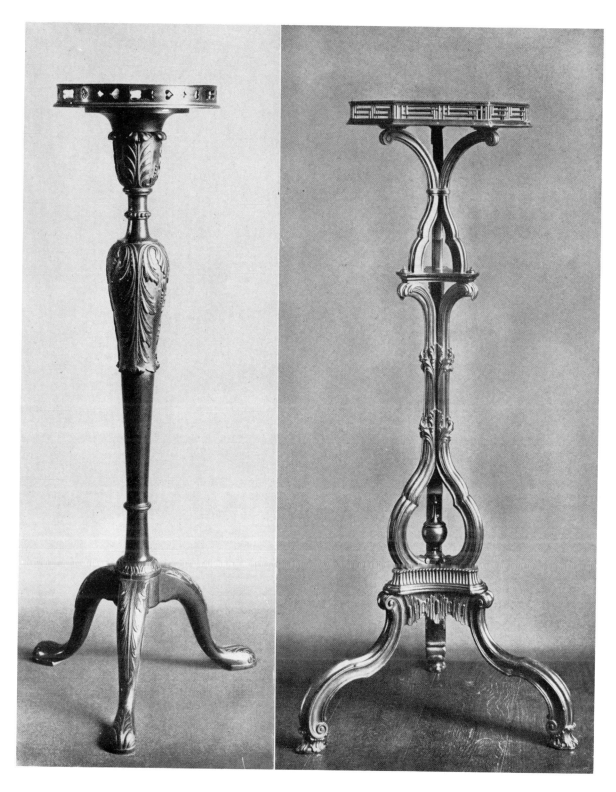

Fig. 197 (left).—Mahogany candle stand on tripod foot.   Circa 1735.   This stand is one of a pair.
Fig. 198 (right).—Mahogany candle stand designed in the chinese-cum-gothic manner.   Circa 1760.
The craftsmanship displayed in the execution of this stand is of the highest quality.

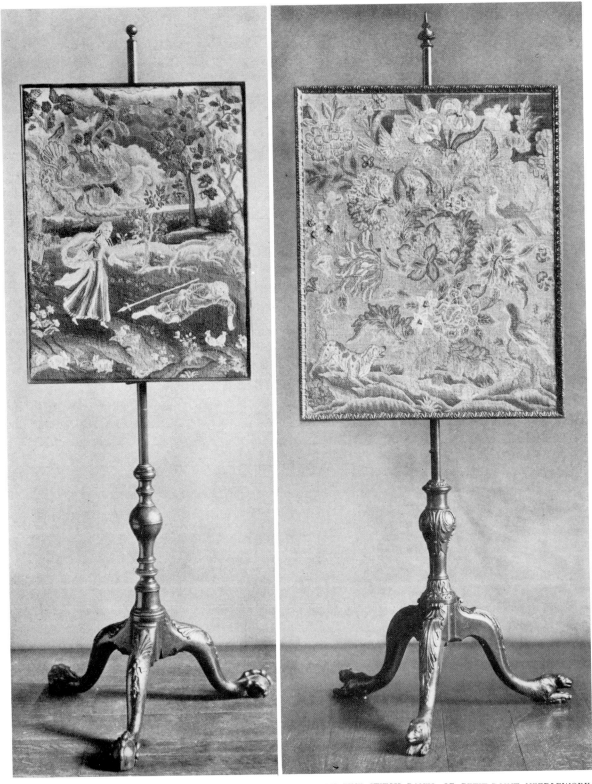

FIG. 199 (LEFT).—FIRE-SCREEN ON WALNUT TRIPOD STAND, WITH FINE STITCH PANEL OF PETIT-POINT NEEDLEWORK.
CIRCA 1730.

FIG. 200 (RIGHT).—FIRE-SCREEN ON MAHOGANY TRIPOD STAND, WITH PANEL OF PETIT-POINT NEEDLEWORK.
A VERY UNUSUAL FEATURE OF THIS EXAMPLE IS THE MOTIF OF A BEAR (FIG. 158), WHICH TERMINATES THE LEGS.
CIRCA 1745.

FIG. 201.—FIRE-SCREEN ON MAHOGANY TRIPOD BASE, WITH THE VERY UNUSUAL DESIGN OF AN EAGLE'S CLAW GRASPING A BLOCK.   THE SCREEN IS COVERED WITH FINE STITCH PETIT-POINT NEEDLEWORK.   CIRCA 1740.

195

Fig. 202.—MAHOGANY DUMB WAITER (IRISH ?).   CIRCA 1735.   THIS PIECE IS NOT ONLY OF EXTREMELY UNUSUAL
DESIGN, BUT THE EXECUTION OF THE CARVING IS OF THE HIGHEST QUALITY.   SEE DETAIL OF LEG, FIG. 159.

FIG. 203.—MAHOGANY TEA URN STAND, WITH SERPENTINE-SHAPED TOP, AND LEGS IN THE FRENCH TASTE. CIRCA 1775.

FIG. 204.—MAHOGANY READING STAND ON TRIPOD BASE. CIRCA 1770.

197

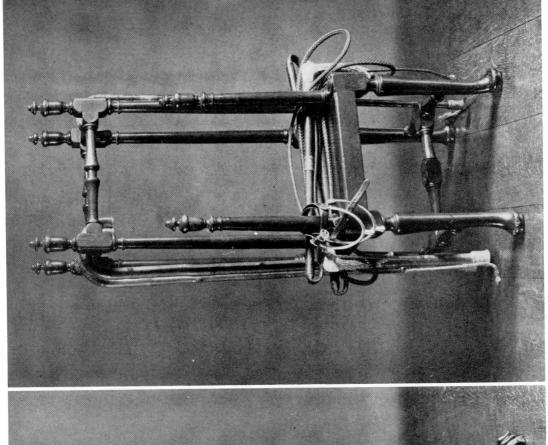

FIG. 206.—MAHOGANY WHIP AND CROP STAND WITH TURNED RAILS AND STRETCHERS.   CIRCA 1740.   THIS IS A VERY UNUSUAL AND RARE PIECE.

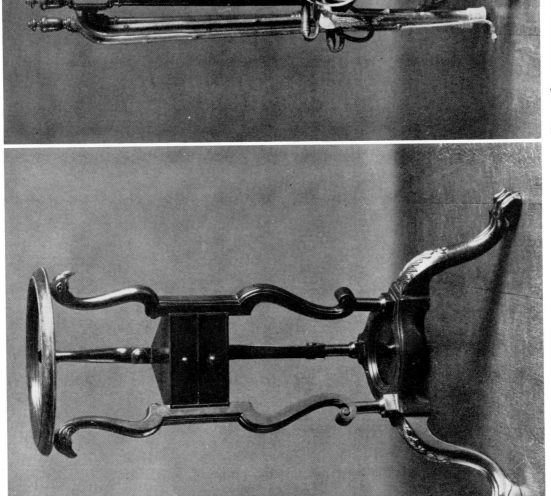

FIG. 205.—MAHOGANY POWDER STAND.   CIRCA 1740.   THIS EXAMPLE WITH THE EAGLE HEAD MOTIF AND CLAW FEET IS VERY UNUSUAL, AS THE MAJORITY OF THESE STANDS ARE OF A QUITE PLAIN DESIGN.

Fig. 208.—MAHOGANY CORNER NIGHT TABLE. CIRCA 1765. THE GADROONED MOULDING TO THE TOP, SIMILAR IN DESIGN TO THE ROOF OF A CHINESE PAGODA, IS A TYPICAL MOTIF OFTEN FOUND ON FURNITURE IN THE CHINESE TASTE.

199

Fig. 207.—MAHOGANY TEAPOY, FITTED WITH ZINC CANSTERS. CIRCA 1765.

Fig. 209.—MAHOGANY BUREAU BOOKCASE WITH UPPER PART OF ARCHITECTURAL DESIGN.   CIRCA 1735.
THIS PIECE IS CHARACTERISTIC OF THE DESIGN OF WILLIAM KENT.

FIG. 210.—MAHOGANY BUREAU BOOKCASE.　　　　CIRCA 1750.　　　　FOR DETAIL, SEE FIG. 149.

Fig. 211.—IRISH MAHOGANY DECANTER STAND.   CIRCA 1750.

NOTICE THE WEBBED CLAW AND BALL FOOT TYPICAL OF IRISH FURNITURE.

202

MIRROR WITH GLASS BORDERS AND CRESTING

Decorated in black and gold *verre eglomisé*

Circa 1700

203

CHAPTER IV.

FAKING.

IT has been declared more than once recently that the art of faking furniture is dying out. A truer statement of the facts would be that the furniture faker finds that what would have deceived the collector five or six years ago can now be instantly recognised as a fake by even the least experienced amateur. Those fakers, therefore, who have not had the skill to improve their art have dropped out of the business of making spurious furniture, while the more ambitious have so procceded to sharpen their wits that they can now produce faked pieces with a skill which will baffle even the most knowledgeable dealer and the most experienced collector. Faking, which is no less than the science of obtaining a living by deception, is persisted in to-day, will no doubt continue to be practised in the future, and that it flourished in the past is borne out by what William Hogarth has to say about picture faking in the middle of the eighteenth century. He writes :—

" Nor have there been wanting of artful people, who have made good profit of those whose unbounded admiration hath run them into enthusiasm. Nay there are, I believe, some who still carry on a comfortable trade in such originals as have been so defaced and maimed by time, that it would be impossible, without a pair of *double-ground* connoisseur-spectacles, to see whether they have ever been good or bad : they deal also in cook'd-up copies, which they are very apt to put off for originals. And whoever dares be bold enough to detect such impositions, finds himself immediately branded, and given out as one of low ideas, ignorant of the true sublime, self-conceited, envious, etc."

" But as there are a great part of mankind that delight most in what they least understand ; for ought I know, the emolument may be equal between the *bubler* and the *bubled* : at least this seems to have been Butler's opinion :

" ' Doubtless the pleasure is as great
In being cheated, as to cheat.' "

The artful faker of to-day does indeed " carry on a comfortable trade " very much in the manner of his eighteenth century predecessor, and at a time even more propitious, owing to the extraordinary increase in the value of old walnut and mahogany furniture, especially of the former. In his more recent work he pays very much more attention than before to constructional details, such as dovetailing and the method of fixing drawer bottoms, for he knows that the collector has begun to study these features and can no longer be deceived by a piece, purporting to be Queen Anne, with drawer bottoms fixed with a grooved fillet, which was a method of construction, as explained on page 158, practised from the last quarter of the eighteenth century. It is all to the good that the collector and the dealer should know about these constructional details, as it gives more trouble to the faker and adds to the cost of his piece by reason of the additional labour involved. He can no longer leave a Victorian drawer in his faked example, but must now entirely reconstruct the drawer in order that it should correspond with the method of construction used in the period to which his fake purports to belong.

To learn how to detect faked furniture requires not only an intimate knowledge of old furniture under the various headings, as laid down on page 14, but also so close a familiarity with the design, craftsmanship and quality of the past schools of cabinet-making that the recognition of old work becomes, as it were, an intuitive sense.

In an old house, the proportio s of the rooms, windows and doors, the design of the chimney-pieces, the panelling and r ouldings, all go to create an atmosphere of the period to which they belong, which clings to and pervades the whole building, and to which the sensitive and knowledgeable mind is susceptible. A modern reproduction of a Queen Anne room will convey no such feeling of atmosphere at all, and will completely lack the subtle significance of the real. In the same way, though in a lesser degree, a piece of old furniture will have atmosphere. This atmosphere is created by the proportion, the design, the ornament, the method of workmanship, and by the natural and eloquent effects of age. Any addition or alteration will tend to destroy the atmosphere, since the difference in character between work carried out as it was originally conceived and that done in a different period and at a later date, will be apparent to the eye and will create an element of discord.

It is not proposed, however, to leave the subject of the detection of fakes on the assumption that the reader has or has not the intuitive sense which will permit him to feel the difference between the atmosphere of a Queen Anne piece of furniture and that of a Victorian one. Until he has studied the subject and gained a complete knowledge of it, he will not realise that in the case of furniture there can be such a thing as atmosphere at all, and may possibly ridicule the very suggestion. If, after careful study, he persists in this view, then it will have to be concluded that his sensibilities are at fault.

The collector, in the course of his researches, will go through a number of phases. One of the first will be a suspicion of every piece; when he will be apt to believe that a genuine example is spurious—a fault common enough among many of those whose knowledge takes them a certain way and no further. Such a collector will for ever be discovering supposed signs of new manufacture ; he will be suspicious of the cleanness of the wood of drawer linings and of the carcase wood, and an absence of signs of wear on the drawer runners will also appear to be convincing proof that a piece is new. Greater experience will enable him to overcome this attitude of scepticism, especially with regard to cleanliness, as he will realise that it is more difficult to reproduce the appearances of age by a clean wooden surface than by a dirty or soiled one. Dirt does not necessarily indicate age, for a piece may be two hundred years old and yet have the drawer interiors as clean looking as when it was first made. Suppose, for instance, the drawers have been locked up for a long period of time, without either having been exposed to the atmosphere or soiled by articles being placed in them. Then, to the inexperienced eye, they will look quite new. This, of course, is an exceptional case, as the interiors of drawers are nearly always dirtied by ordinary use.

Having passed through this initial stage of mistrust, the collector will then be filled with over-confidence, and will enthusiastically praise as a rare piece an example hot from the faker's studio. After he has experienced much bitter disillusionment, he will realise that the craft of the faker is not to be despised, and that to detect a really good fake will require the keenest perception, backed by considerable knowledge and experience.

He will learn how fatal it is to rely on first impressions, and how important it is that every portion of a piece should be brought under a long and close scrutiny in strong daylight. He will also find that a strong magnifying glass will reveal much that is not apparent to the naked eye. The skilled and experienced faker, who will benefit to the extent of several hundred pounds if he makes a faked piece good enough to deceive, will leave no stone unturned to ensure immunity for his piece. It behoves the collector, therefore, to use all possible care in his analysis of a piece before coming to a definite decision, and not to be over-confident, as it is this very confidence which encompasses his downfall and permits the faker to reap his illegitimate gains.

THE RECONSTRUCTION OF OLD PIECES.

The efforts of the skilled faker to-day are more directed towards the alteration and adaptation of genuine pieces than the making of entirely new ones. To adapt a piece which, owing to its design, is unsaleable and therefore of comparatively little value, and alter it into a saleable and more valuable example, is a much more paying proposition. The chances of detection are considerably lessened because the greater part of such a piece is genuine. As an example of this type of adaptation, the following may be cited. A walnut bureau bookcase with solid walnut doors to the upper part is worth at least two-thirds less than an example with mirror panels to the doors. The alteration of the doors into panelled mirror doors can be carried out quite easily and satisfactorily at a cost of £15 to £20. The result is an increase in value of perhaps £100 or £150. Very little new material is required in this alteration, and, in consequence, the amount of freshly cut surface that requires faking will be small. Another example is that of a piece of walnut which is sometimes found with a tall glazed upper part and a secretaire and drawers underneath. Such a piece is of tall proportions, and the secretaire is quite useless. It is by no means a difficult task to remove the secretaire part and reconstruct the drawers underneath it to form a base for the upper part, which is left entirely in its original condition. This subtraction results in a well proportioned, rare and most saleable bookcase or china cabinet. In its original form it was most probably unsaleable or worth at most £200; whereas in its new form it will be worth £800.

Another method of making a china cabinet is to turn the solid doors of a walnut cabinet, supported on a base with drawers, into glazed doors formed of rectangular panels of clear glass. In this reconstruction the depth of the cabinet is also reduced, as, in their original form, these solid door cabinets are bulky and rather useless pieces of furniture, for which there is no great demand. After their conversion into shallow china cabinets the faker finds a ready market with some unsuspicious customer.

Another piece which lends itself to reconstruction is the high pedestal writing desk with a sloping top. These desks were made for business offices, the writer sitting on a high stool. Quite a number of them have survived in mahogany, and some examples are of an elaborate character, with mouldings enriched by carving. As desks, four feet in height, they are practically unsaleable. No collector could find a utilitarian purpose for a piece of this description in his house. By carefully removing the desk portion, taking away a drawer from each pedestal and fitting a new top lined with leather, a flat-topped pedestal writing table, one of the rarest and most sought-after pieces of antique furniture that is to be found to-day, is cunningly evolved. The difference in value between the two is several hundred per cent.; well worth the outlay of the £30 or £40 necessary for the metamorphosis.

There are many other reconstructions of this nature. A favourite one with the faker—although not of an English piece—is the conversion of the walnut Dutch wardrobe with solid doors, which is practically unsaleable, into a china cabinet with the doors glazed in small rectangular panes. In this alteration the depth of the wardrobe is reduced, as the china cabinet was always shallow. As the English walnut china cabinet is almost unknown, the Dutch china cabinet has considerably increased in value within recent years. This increase in value and continued demand has resulted in hitherto unsaleable Dutch wardrobes being eagerly bought up by the faker, and as rapidly as possible converted into china cabinets. This means to-day that the value of a piece, worth £10 or £15, has risen to £40 or £50, or, in the case of a very good example of small dimensions, to perhaps £80.

Another profitable undertaking of the faker is the alteration of continental furniture, usually Dutch or German walnut pieces, by removing the strongly marked characteristics of their *provenance* so that they will resemble English ones. Heavy mouldings of straight run walnut will be removed and replaced by those of a lighter section and cross-grained. Knowledge of the methods of construction, material and the quality of workmanship of these continental pieces will easily prevent a purchaser from being imposed upon by this form of deception.

The small long-case clock, commonly known as a " grandmother," is of the greatest rarity, and is also one of the most sought-after pieces, both by the clock and the furniture collector. The rarity of the genuine article gives the faker an opening for making spurious ones, which he does by reconstructing the late eighteenth century wall clock in a mahogany case, similar in design to the fine lacquer example illustrated (fig. 212). By merely adding a plinth, he converts a rather unsaleable clock, worth perhaps £20 or £30, into one that he easily disposes of for £200 or £300. The scarcity of the genuine specimen should be sufficient to put the collector on his guard against any example that may be offered to him. These reconstructed clocks are generally smaller than the genuine grandmother clock.

One further reconstruction is that of the sofa table, the demand for which is considerable both here and in America. The sofa table that is sought after is the type that has curved legs at each end and a stretcher connecting them. This table is growing extremely scarce, and the faker therefore converts the table which has an exactly similar top—but instead of being supported by legs at each end, is supported on a central pedestal with four curved legs—into the more saleable example. He uses the curved portion of the legs of the pedestal for the new legs, the upper part of the legs and the stretcher alone being of new material.

A deception often practised by the faker with regard to bureau bookcases is to " marry "—as it is termed in the trade—an old upper part, which he has found divorced

FIG. 212 (LEFT).—HANGING WALL CLOCK IN BLACK AND GOLD LACQUER CASE WITH MOVEMENT BY EDWARD MOORE, OXFORD.   CIRCA 1740.

FIG. 213 (RIGHT).—WHEEL BAROMETER IN WALNUT CASE, BY J. HALLIFAX, BARNSLEY.   CIRCA 1740.

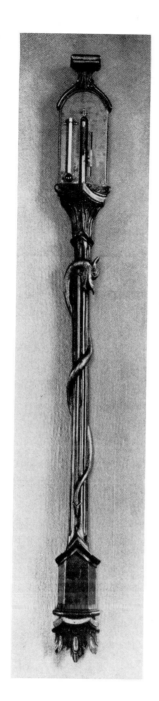

Fig. 214 (left).—Mahogany and gilt barometer, signed S. Tod, Edinburgh.   circa 1765.

Fig. 215 (right).—A rare type of wheel barometer, by John Whitehurst, Derby, in walnut standing case of design similar to a clock case.   height, 4 feet 6 inches.   circa 1760.

from its lower half, to an old bureau.   In such a piece both the upper and lower portions will be genuine. The difficulty the faker has to overcome is to find a bureau the top of which is of exactly the right dimensions to take the upper part.   The depth is not so important, as he can usually reduce the depth of the bookcase, but the width must be more or less correct.   He will fix a cross-grained moulding along the front and two sides of the top to take the upper part.   Sometimes, when the bureau is not of exactly the right measurements for the upper part, he will make good the discrepancy by making the moulding narrow or wide, as the case may be.   If the moulding, therefore, on the top of a bureau that encloses the bookcase portion is narrower or wider than is usually the case on a genuine bureau, the piece can then be regarded with mistrust, especially if the polish also has the appearance of being faked.   The surface of the top of the bureau should be examined for any signs of a toothing plane, as originally it will have been covered with veneer, which, of course, will have been removed.

It may be argued that these reconstructed pieces are not fakes, but are genuine antiques, since the greater part of the material is old.   This argument, however, cannot hold good ; for, to sell pieces of this description as genuine, and at the price that they would fetch if they were, is fraudulent.   Furthermore, the intrinsic value of such genuine pieces lies fundamentally in their design, which, in the case of the reconstruction, is not original.

The faker is always using his brains to discover how to make objects for which there is an immediate sale and constant demand, from pieces which he can buy cheaply, and which, because of their design, are unsaleable.   It is, of course, justifiable to sell such pieces under their proper description as altered pieces ; but it is doubtful whether, in this case, the faker would find it worth his while to convert such pieces for the small profit that they would earn.   The collector can never be certain whether he is confronted with a reconstructed piece or not, because, although the examples cited are of the usual run of conversions, it is quite possible that a faker may find some unusual article which, even if ugly in form, lends itself, or some portion of it, to adaptation.   He is always on the look out for pieces that can be reconstructed in this way.

An analogous practice with regard to chairs is the conversion of the commode chair into the ordinary chair by cutting away the deep apron pieces of the seat rails.   This is a less harmful procedure, since the operation does not affect the design to the same extent.

FAKED PIECES OF NEW CONSTRUCTION MADE FROM OLD MATERIAL.

In making an entirely new piece the faker is confronted with a considerably harder proposition.   The difficulty is not so much in the faking of the external polished surface of the piece, as the unpolished surface of the interior of the carcase, the drawer linings, and, in the case of chairs, the insides of the seat rails.   The unpolished surface of old oak, deal, pine or beech, which has become dry and mature through age, is impossible to reproduce on freshly cut wood.

The deal forming the carcases of pieces of walnut and mahogany often has a very fresh and clean appearance.   This, however, applies to the portions of the carcase that are not exposed, such as the sides and dust-boards.   Where the deal is exposed, such as in the case of the back board, it will be of a dark tone, caused by dust and dirt having worked into the surface in the course of a number of years.

A peculiarity that belongs to an old deal or pine surface, and which is a definite sign of age when it occurs, is that the annular rings stand out owing to the shrinkage of the softer fibre between them.   This, however, is not so noticeable on the unexposed parts of the carcase of a piece as it is on the underneath framing of a table or on the boards forming the back of a bureau or chest-with-drawers, which are open to the atmosphere.

FIG. 216.—WALNUT BUREAU.   CIRCA 1730.   THE FRONT IS VENEERED WITH BURR WALNUT, AND THE DRAWER LININGS ARE OF OAK.

In examining any piece, the colour and surface condition of the unpolished wood are what require the closest scrutiny.   If the wood of the carcase or drawer linings, or of the seat rails to chairs, presents a foggy or stained appearance, suspicion should be at once aroused.   Knowing full well the difficulty of treating successfully the unpolished soft wood, the faker endeavours where possible to use old wood, carefully preserving its matured surface.   This old wood he obtains from derelict carcases of chests-with-drawers and tallboys—sometimes of walnut —too far gone to be restored, of which the wood is more valuable than the pieces themselves.   Early Victorian furniture is another source of supply.   Some fakers will also import Dutch furniture to break up, as the oak used in the drawers and carcases of Dutch pieces is of the finest quality and admirably suited for the drawer linings and carcases of their work.

In order to detect a new piece of deal or oak, a very simple test is to cut a small chip from the surface with a penknife, and if the wood is new it will be of a much lighter tone where it has been cut, than if it were old. This is a very useful test to apply to the carcase or drawer linings of a piece, if the appearance of the surface of the wood suggests that it has been treated or faked. The same test is applicable to a mahogany piece.

In a spurious example of new construction where old deal has been employed, the colour and surface of the deal may not be the same throughout the piece. This is specially noticeable when two boards join each other, such as when they form the back board of a piece or the underneath of a table top. In an old piece this does not occur, as the deal would all have been newly cut when the piece was made, and consequently will have matured to the same extent. The above remarks also apply to oak.

The spurious walnut piece usually has the carcase made of oak, and not of deal. This is partly because the faker can more readily obtain old oak, and partly because, if he is forced to cut or resurface the oak, he can fake it to a better colour than he can deal.

In making pieces of entirely new construction, the faker's work is much more open to detection, and, therefore, if he does aspire to produce an example of this kind, he will choose a piece to imitate which is small in size and of considerable value. In the last two or three years there has been a considerable demand for the small bureau on cabriole legs, similar to the example illustrated (fig. 216). Owing to this demand, these pieces have risen sufficiently in value to make the construction of a spurious example a very paying proposition. Carcases and drawer linings will be constructed entirely of wood obtained from old pieces ; the matured surface of the wood in each case being carefully preserved. For the exterior he will sometimes use old, and sometimes modern, walnut veneer. The narrow walnut bureau bookcase (see fig. 33) is another type of bureau of which the faker finds it profitable to make spurious examples. This kind of deception generally takes the form of constructing the upper part out of old wood, usually of a design similar to the type with a single mirror-panelled door. The faked upper part is made to fit a genuine bureau. For the mirror of the door he will prefer to use an old plate with its original bevelled edges, if he is able to find one of suitable dimensions. The fact that the bureau is genuine is a great help in deceiving the purchaser. The sides of the upper part and the sides of the bureau should be examined, to see whether there is any variation in the colour and polish. The back boards of the upper and lower parts should also be examined for any difference in colour.

Another trick of the faker, to increase the value of a bureau bookcase, is to make an interior fitment for the upper part with drawers and pigeon-holes and a central cupboard, as an example with such a fitment is always of considerably more value than if it had plain shelves. The high quality workmanship as displayed in the drawers of a genuine example is seldom reproduced by the faker. The very thin drawer sides, usually of walnut, skilfully rabbetted to take the flush bottom, and the fine dovetailing, are features that, to copy accurately, would make this fitment too expensive an addition for a profit to result.

A piece of rarity and high value of which the faker will make imitations of new construction is the bachelor chest with folding top, similar to examples, figs. 115 and 116. The walnut card table is another piece which he reproduces for similar reasons. Sometimes he will make an example to fit a piece of old *petit-point* needlework, which was originally worked for a card table, since a table with a *petit-point* top of a design of playing cards and counters is of the greatest rarity. Spurious walnut tripod tables also have their tops fitted with old needlework panels, which are contained usually in borders of cross-banded walnut. Any table which is described as having its original needlework top should always be looked upon with the gravest mistrust, as it is only one example in a thousand that will be genuine both as regards the table and the needlework.* Sometimes spurious needlework is made to fit an old table, but it is generally the reverse. Owing to the scarcity and high value of eighteenth century English needlework, the faker often uses that of continental *provenance,* which is much coarser in stitch and cruder in colouring.

DRAWERS AND THEIR LININGS.

The faker is specially skilled in making a new drawer from an old one. In this new drawer, the only freshly cut wood that will be visible is the end grain of the dovetails and that of the pin pieces. In examining a drawer, therefore, this end grain should be carefully scrutinised to see whether there is any sign of the wood having been newly cut, and whether it shows signs of recent staining when compared with the drawer sides. It is the cut edges of the wood that should be examined, and not the surface. When the edge shows a variation in colour to that of the surface, which is more noticeable on the long grain than on the end grain, suspicion should be at once aroused.

The carcase of a spurious piece, especially the dust-boards, is often treated with a coat of wax which is then covered with dust. This trick is frequently resorted to when the wood has a freshly cut surface, as the dust will help to obscure it. If the dust is removed by a damp cloth, the new surface of the wood will be at once disclosed.

In order to wear down the runners of a newly made drawer and the surface of the dust-board on which the drawer rests, the faker places heavy weights inside the drawer and keeps on working it in and out until both the dust-board and the runners are worn.

Careful examination should be made of the dovetails, as constantly in a faked piece they will be badly fitted with open joints between the pin and the dovetail. This method of making a dovetail is purposely done in order to give an appearance of age. The faker, however, generally makes too wide and even a crack around the dovetail, which looks artificial and has not the natural appearance of old dovetailing, where a crack, when one does occur between the pin and the dovetail, is generally caused by shrinkage and not through defective workmanship. Knowledge of the different methods of dovetailing and the fixing of drawer bottoms in the various periods, as explained in Chapter II., will also be useful for detecting spurious work.

---

* Sometimes a genuine panel of needlework will be fitted on to a genuine table, but this can only very seldom be done owing to the difficulty of finding a table with a top of the correct size.

One other point concerning dovetails. The dovetailing should, throughout the piece, be of the same type : that is, the dovetails to the drawers in the upper part of a chest on stand, and those in the drawers of the stand itself. If there is any variation, it strongly points to the fact that all the drawers are not contemporary. The skilled faker is aware of this, and, therefore, seldom makes a mistake of this kind. The same remarks also apply to the methods of fixing drawer bottoms. The wood of the drawer fronts and linings should also be the same throughout a piece.

The wood of drawer linings should be carefully examined for any sign of previous use. A drawer bottom will often show grooved lines, which have been made by the pins which hold the stops having become exposed by the wood being worn away. If, therefore, a drawer bottom is grooved in this manner and the grooves do not correspond to the drawer stops, suspicion should be aroused, because it points to the fact that the wood used for the drawer linings once formed the linings to another drawer.

Sometimes, to avoid the necessity of faking the linings of a drawer, the faker will paste blue paper over them after the manner in which drawers were lined in the eighteenth century. Another trick, intended to convey the impression of age, is to paste an old newspaper in a drawer or at the back of a mirror. For this reason the value of old newspapers has risen.

VENEER, AND CROSS-GRAINED MOULDINGS.

In using modern veneer, the skilled faker will have it saw cut and of a thickness equal to the old. In the process of sandpapering and rubbing down the surface he will eradicate the curved lines made by the circular saw with which modern veneers are cut ; the presence of which is quite sufficient proof that the piece is modern. If he be very conscientious, he will also remove them from the underneath side of the veneer by toothing it with a toothing plane before laying it down on the carcase ; as, if he does not do this, they may possibly show through the thickness of the veneer, if it is thin and has received much sandpapering on its outer surface. The old veneer was sawn by hand, which marked the surface with straight though not parallel lines.

Knife-cut veneer, which is veneer cut by the modern method, is much thinner than saw-cut, and is sometimes used in the manufacture of cheap imitations because it can very easily be bleached to a good colour by reason of its thinness. Care has to be taken in the rubbing down to avoid going right through it. A piece veneered with knife-cut veneer can, of course, be adjudged spurious.

The cross-grained mouldings on an old piece will often exhibit cracks running the way of the grain. These cracks are caused through shrinkage. The faker imitates them by damping the walnut before he glues it down on the soft wood core. The walnut is cut as thin as is compatible with the surface being planed to the required section. The moulding is then put into a hot oven, when the heat will cause the walnut to shrink, and, in contracting, curl up and crack in the same manner as the old mouldings were affected. What the action of time took fifty years to bring about, the faker accomplishes in as many hours.

RE-VENEERING OLD PIECES.

An example of how the faker sometimes overcomes the difficulty presented by the unpolished wood of the carcase and of the drawer linings is illustrated in cases where he makes a spurious walnut writing table from a Victorian one of oak. This he does by veneering the exterior surfaces of the latter with walnut, and making new mouldings of correct section in cross-grained wood. In order to make this deception more complete, he will alter the Victorian method of fixing the drawer bottoms with a grooved fillet, and instead make rabbetted drawer bottoms with runners, which, as already explained, was the method employed in the eighteenth century. If by any chance he does not do this, then a walnut pedestal writing table, if found with its drawer bottoms fixed with a grooved fillet, can be at once condemned as not being a period example. A large number of spurious walnut tables of this description have been turned out by the faker quite recently, as walnut pedestal writing tables are of the greatest rarity, and there is considerable competition for them among collectors. The faker finds such a conversion an extremely paying proposition, as a table of this kind costs under £100 to produce, and, even when sold at half the price it would fetch if genuine, will still reap a profit of several hundred pounds.

Besides the Victorian writing table, the faker also transforms the lower-grade oak furniture dating from the first half of the eighteenth century into veneered walnut examples. The only new parts will be the veneer and the cross-grained mouldings. The back boards, the interior of the carcase and the drawer linings will be original and of the correct construction, but the carcase will naturally be of oak and not of deal. The period walnut piece with an oak carcase, as already mentioned, is not only of extreme rarity, but is of the highest quality workmanship. This latter feature will certainly not be found in a lower-grade oak piece, especially as regards the dovetailed work and the fitting of the drawer bottoms. Knowledge of the various grades of quality of craftsmanship on the part of the collector will always be of considerable help in detecting the old oak piece with its exterior surface overlaid with modern walnut veneer. This trick of veneering old pieces with walnut is a very favourite one with the faker at the present time, owing to the demand for, and rarity of the genuine example.

THE FAKER'S METHODS OF POLISHING.

After long experiment, the faker is now able to imitate the colour and polish of old walnut very successfully. In the early days of faking walnut, he was unable to obtain the golden colour because he obscured the surface of the wood with stain and polish. To-day his polish is clear and transparent, and this achievement is one of the reasons why the faked walnut piece is now such a serious menace to the collector. Between the original piece and the faked example, however, there is still this difference. The colour of old walnut, as already explained, is caused through the mellowing of the varnish ; but in a faked example this colour is given to the wood before it is polished. This is achieved by placing the piece in a fume chamber, when it has left the cabinet-maker's hands and is ready for polishing. In a fume chamber both the inner and outer surfaces of the piece come into contact with acid fumes, which bleach out the black grain of the walnut, and turn the grey tone into brown. Thus, when the piece is polished, all the harshness and dark grain of the modern walnut is converted into the golden brown tone of the old. A fume chamber is not always employed, but it is by far the most satisfactory method, as the piece that is left in fumes of specially prepared acids for a period of two or three days will have the whole of its surfaces, including the carcase wood and the drawer linings, affected. Fakers who do not use a fume chamber apply the acid direct on to the wood. After the acid has achieved the desired result, its action must be stopped, which is usually done with vinegar, as otherwise it will rot the wood and will keep on coming out in the form of a white mold for many months afterwards. The white mold formed by the acid working out is sometimes noticeable on the deal back of a piece, or on the seat rail of a chair.

Spurious mahogany furniture is also treated in the same manner, except that the acids employed are of a different character. The effect of fuming on mahogany is to take the red colour out of the wood and give it the brown shade of old mahogany.

If a mahogany piece, before it is polished, is exposed to the air and sunlight, the same effect will be produced ; the red will be bleached out of the wood, and, in addition, the surface will become mature and considerably help the process of polishing. Fakers who can afford to make pieces and keep them in an unpolished state for six months or a year often do this with highly beneficial results.

Some of the more experienced fakers, who are constantly experimenting to produce the exact colour of old walnut and mahogany, are trying the effect of bleaching the surface of the wood with ultra-violet rays. What must be still more disquieting to the collector of the future is that experiments are now taking place to endeavour to mellow the varnish, thus changing the colour of the wood after the piece has been polished in exactly the same way as the old walnut furniture altered under the natural processes of time and exposure.

Fakers, however, guard their secrets very jealously, and work behind closed doors. The only way of finding out their methods is to study their handiwork on completion. Not only do they seek to safeguard their secrets, but each keeps his own particular recipes to himself and does not share his knowledge with his fellow rogues.

Undoubtedly each faker has his own particular method of polishing, but shellac polish would appear to be the one generally used. A number of coats of it are applied, and after each coat it is well rubbed down with rotten-stone. This partial removal of the polish after its application, not only helps to fill up the grain of the wood, but the constant rubbing gives the surface a patinated appearance.

In order to imitate the dark tone of the background and of the interstices of the carving —so noticeable a feature of the old piece, as described on page 15 —boot blacking or dirtied wax is well rubbed in with a hard brush. Sometimes this light and shade effect on the carving is obtained by applying a dark spirit stain, after the surface has been polished. The stain is then wiped off from the high lights, but left in the interstices, thus obtaining a very good imitation of the effect so typical of the original piece. If, however, this

s

FIG. 217.—DETAIL OF TOP OF WALNUT CARD TABLE, FIG. 25.
SEE ALSO FAKED TOP, FIG. 218.

staining is examined through a magnifying glass, its presence on the surface—especially on a light wood like walnut—can more often than not be detected, unless it has been done with exceptional skill. After the application of the shellac polish, the piece is then well waxed and finished with a dull surface.

In the case of mahogany furniture which is carved, the surface is sometimes given a coat of varnish, which fills up the grain and gives a good body to the wood for the shellac polish which is afterwards applied. There is much more difficulty in filling up the grain of mahogany than walnut. Soft mahogany, too, does not take the fumes so well as the hard. The faker, therefore, will always use old Spanish or Cuban mahogany for his work whenever possible, as, not only is it easier to obtain a better colour in these woods, but they are also easier to polish. In making a mahogany example, the faker will endeavour to form the outer surfaces from pieces of old mahogany with their original polished surface, for which purpose he buys up tops of old dining tables and old mahogany fitments, such as shop and office counters. If he cuts old mahogany, the new surface, when polished, will be a red colour. He will, therefore, have to fume it in order to give it a brown tone. Old mahogany is not only of far superior quality to the modern, but it will be seasoned by age and will be darker. This applies, not only to the outer surface, but to the thickness of a plank throughout.

Both walnut and mahogany fakes are sometimes treated with a thick coat of varnish, which is stained a dark colour and gives the surface of the piece a treacly appearance. The varnish is often cracked and blistered by heat to make it look more convincingly old. Such a treatment is carried out by the faker because many genuine walnut and mahogany pieces have survived in this condition, owing to their having been given a coat

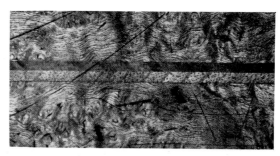

FIG. 218.—PORTION OF WALNUT VENEER WITH HERRING-BONE INLAY, TAKEN FROM A FAKED PIECE.
NOTICE THE ABSENCE OF DARK LINES ON EACH SIDE OF HERRING-BONE INLAY AS COMPARED WITH FIG. 217.

of oil varnish, which was a subsequent treatment by an unskilled hand to renovate the surface of the piece.   The faker rightly imagines that an intending purchaser will mistake his piece for an original one which has been subsequently varnished in this manner, hoping that, by the skilful removal of the varnish, the original polished surface of the piece will be disclosed underneath.   In such a case, however, the purchaser will find too late that, when the varnish is removed, a freshly cut mahogany or walnut surface will be revealed. Sometimes, in order to hide freshly cut mahogany, the surface will be coated with dark-coloured wax which is burnt and blistered.   Wax of this description is much softer than that on an original piece, although the faker hardens it with gold size.   When this kind of dirtied wax is scraped off with a knife, the freshly cut wood will be found underneath.

In detecting the work of a clever faker, especially with regard to walnut, the polish will be found to present considerable difficulty, since pieces polished in the manner already described, with shellac, bear a very close resemblance to the old pieces treated with shellac varnish.   They will not, however, resemble the highly polished varnished piece, as they will usually have a surface with an eggshell gloss.   One distinguishing difference between the old piece and the modern that is often, but not invariably present, is that in the old example which has its original polish, dark lines will be found where the herring-bone banding joins the veneer (fig. 217).   This is caused by the glue coming through the join, which is opened through shrinkage.   In a piece with modern veneer, these dark lines will seldom be present (fig. 218).   By itself, this test is not, of course, conclusive; but is useful when employed in conjunction with other confirmatory evidence.

In modern herring-bone banding the grain of the wood will often have been bleached by the acid to such an extent that there will be hardly any grain perceptible.   In the majority of old pieces, the grain of this banding can be clearly seen.   In modern work, where one piece of veneer joins another, as, for example, on the top of a table, the join is open and not filled up with polish.   In the case of a table with its original polish, this will not be so, except where the veneer has come away from the carcase wood and the edges have curled up, owing to the glue perishing either through damp or heat.   This last-named state is imitated by the faker on his spurious pieces by damping the veneer and heating it with hot coils or irons.   This causes the veneer to shrink and curl up. Dirtied wax, hardened with gold size, is then rubbed into the cracks to imitate beeswax hardened by age.

In a spurious walnut piece, such as a table, the top will sometimes be bleached a light colour to imitate a feature often found on the genuine example.   This bleached colour is not caused by the perishing of the polish, as explained on page 103, but by chemical action on the wood itself.

Genuine pieces of walnut which are of a dark colour are to-day not so saleable as those of a light faded colour.   In order, therefore, to appreciate the value of the former, the faker strips off the original polish, bleaches the surface of the walnut veneer to a lighter colour, and then repolishes it.   It may be argued that this is not faking in the true sense of the word, but a legitimate improvement.   At the same time, unless the procedure is disclosed to the intending purchaser, it is increasing the value of a piece by artificial means, and thereby securing a sale by a fraudulent artifice.

SURFACE EXAMINATION.

One very useful test in the detection of faked furniture consists in the careful, even microscopic examination of the indentations and scratches on the exterior surface of a piece. This can be done best by examining the piece with its surface facing upwards, between the observer and a strong electric light, so that the light falls on it obliquely. The surface of an old piece, especially when of a soft wood such as walnut, when viewed in this way will show an amazing number of indentations and scratches which will be hardly noticeable when the surface is not looked at from an angle. The surface of a drawer will often show a number of minute indentations round the key-hole, caused by the drawer having been locked and unlocked numberless times by a key on a bunch, the other keys, knocking against the wood, having made a number of indentations contained in a small arc. The bottom drawer of a bureau will show a number of scratches where its surface has been kicked. The top of a walnut table will display a number of scratches, indentations and marks, caused in various ways during many years of use. The framing around the drawer openings of the small drawers which are situated at the top of a tallboy will have a number of indentations caused by the top drawer being frequently taken out, since it was too high to see into, and, on being replaced, permitted to strike against the surrounding surface.

These natural signs of wear will, of course, not be present on a piece of modern manufacture, and, so far, the faker has not gone to the trouble of making a study of these marks and of reproducing them accurately.

A spurious table top, when examined, may show a number of deeply gouged scratches and marks on its surface, but their artificial origin will become immediately apparent when compared with the network of indentations, scratches and bruises on an old top, supposing the two are placed side by side. The former look as if they had been done hurriedly and at haphazard. The scratches also will usually be of the same width and the same character, showing that they have all been done at the same time and by the same instrument*.

On an old surface there are many and various types of scratches and indentations. Some of the earlier ones will hardly be perceptible, because they will have been nearly eradicated by the subsequent rubbing and domestic polishing of the surface.

The faker is also aware of the indentations around the key-holes, but, up to the present, his imitations of these marks are palpably artificial when compared with those on the genuine piece.

One difference between these marks on a spurious piece and those on a genuine one is that the faker makes his on the surface of the wood before he applies the polish. If he made them afterwards, he would merely damage the surface of the polish without securing for his marks the semblance of age. The scratches on the polish of a genuine

* The faker sometimes produces marks by jangling a bunch of old keys against the wood, as he knows by doing this that no two indentations will be exactly similar.

walnut surface will show up dark owing to beeswax and dirt having accumulated and hardened. This darkening of scratches is obtained by the faker by filling them with stain and polish.

It may be said that what has been written above will draw the attention of the faker to these shortcomings in his work, and that, in consequence, he will in future so closely reproduce the genuine scratches and indentations that these will cease to constitute a test. This is all to the good, however, as it will cause him more time, trouble and expense.

Another important reason why the surface of a piece should be examined is because, in the case of mahogany, as has already been stated, the faker will use old wood with its original surface. This surface may show marks which it received when in its original form. An illuminating example of this can be instanced. A spurious four-tiered circular revolving bookcase on a tripod stand was examined. The top, which was about 18 inches in diameter and about 5 feet from the ground, showed distinct marks made by a wheel pattern marker. This was undoubted proof that at some time or other dressmaking patterns had been marked out on it. As its present height, 5 feet from the ground, and its small area make it extremely improbable that anyone would have chosen something so inconvenient for such a purpose, it can be safely assumed, therefore, that the top of this bookcase originally formed part of the top of a table.

The appearance on the side of a china cabinet of pot rings, caused by the burning of the wood by a hot vessel, is sufficient proof that the wood was once used in a horizontal position and not a vertical one. A pot ring on a table top which is cut in half by the gallery surmounting it is a seeming enigma which can be explained only by the assumption that the top must once have been larger, and is proof that the table was made from old wood, and is therefore fraudulent.

Careful examination of the wood for signs of previous use should always be made, as this is one of the difficulties the faker has to overcome when making a piece out of old material. For this reason, he finds it much easier to make a small piece than a large one, as, in the case of the former, he is able to cut down and choose his material, while in a large piece he cannot pick and choose.

The presence of any small pieces of wood let into the surface, ostensibly for the purpose of repairing, especially when on the edge, should be viewed with suspicion, as they generally denote that the wood was once used in another form ; the pieces let in being to repair the wood where it had originally been cut to receive a hinge or a lock. If no possible solution can be arrived at for the presence of repairs of this description, it can safely be assumed that the piece is spurious, as the eighteenth century cabinet-maker never employed defective timber, nor any which had been used before, to make his furniture.

One important test to discover whether a mahogany piece possesses its original surface is to examine it with the light behind it and at an angle, as already explained on page 219. The spurious piece will then sometimes disclose the open grain in places where it has not been filled up by the polish. This open grain resembles minute indentations on the surface. Where the polish has covered the wood the surface will be perfectly smooth, and will, in fact, appear like a film over the wood. In an old piece, with its original polish, the surface will show no sign whatsoever of open grain. Indeed, in some cases there will be minute ridges standing out of the grain, which are most probably formed by the oil with which the piece was originally polished being forced out of the wood by shrinkage and becoming solidified. It should be noticed that such ridges only occur on the unexposed portions of a piece, which would not have received a great deal of domestic rubbing.

A piece can still be perfectly genuine and yet disclose open grain, the reason being that its surface may have been stripped and repolished. Careful examination of a surface for signs of this open grain will often show whether any parts are of modern restoration.

An old mahogany surface will be unobscured by any artificial film of polish, because it was polished with oil or wax, as explained on page 170 (*seq.*). The faker, however, seldom polishes his mahogany pieces with brickdust and oil, partly because it is too expensive as regards labour, and partly because he cannot fake the surface and fill up the grain as satisfactorily as he can with shellac polish.

Because of the difficulty of filling up the grain of mahogany, it is easier to distinguish the spurious piece made of that wood than is the case with walnut. The comparison, side by side, of the surfaces of a spurious piece with a genuine one will reveal considerably more than the written word can convey.

TESTS FOR GENUINENESS AS REGARDS HANDLES AND SCREWS.

A blunder which would not be committed by the skilful faker of to-day, but which has often been made in the past, is when an old drawer front, which has holes pierced through it where the original handles were once fixed, has been veneered and the holes covered up, the faker having omitted to pierce the surface of the veneer to correspond with the holes which can be seen at the back of the drawer front.

The skilful faker uses old locks and hinges on his piece, and also goes to the trouble of using hand-made screws for which he is always on the look out, and which he extracts from genuine pieces after he has broken them up. The difference between a hand and a machine-made screw is shown in examples illustrated (fig. 219). It should be noted that the former does not taper.

Screws made prior to 1760 had the threads filed by hand and sometimes had slightly pointed heads (see fig. 219A). After 1760, the thread was cut in a power-driven lathe, the tools being operated by hand. Such screws had blunt heads, and the thread was entirely different to that of the earlier hand-filed screw (see fig. 219C). The machine-made screw with the " gimlet pointed " head (see fig. 219B) was first shown at the Great Exhibition of 1851, and it was not until a few years later that they came into general use.

In a genuine piece of walnut or mahogany furniture dating up to 1760, the screws should be of the hand-filed type, similar to fig. 219A. If a piece is found with the later kind, fig. 219C, it is evidence that it was made in the last half of the eighteenth century,

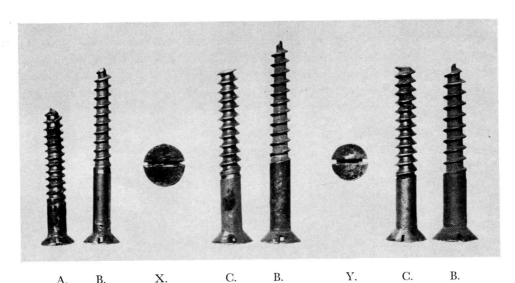

A.   B.   X.   C.   B.   Y.   C.   B.

FIG. 219.—A.—A HAND-FILED SCREW MADE PRIOR TO 1760.
B.—MACHINE-MADE SCREWS DATING FROM 1851 TO PRESENT TIME.
C.—LATHE-MADE SCREWS DATING FROM 1760-1850.
X.—TOP OF LATHE-MADE SCREW.
Y.—TOP OF MACHINE-MADE SCREW.

although not conclusive, as it would not be an unusual occurrence for screws, especially those which are used to fix the locks and hinges, to have been renewed at a later date. In many cases when the faker has no old screws, he will doctor the machine-made screw by cutting off the point, filing down the thread and rusting its surface. The presence of a hand-made screw, therefore, is not a proof that the piece is old, nor conversely, is a machine-made screw found in an apparently old piece proof that the piece is not genuine, as the screws, as already pointed out, may have been removed for some reason or other at a later date and replaced by the then modern screw.

An extremely good test, in order to detect a modern faked piece, is to see if all the screws of the hinges and locks can be unscrewed quite easily. If so, they have undoubtedly been recently inserted. A hand-made screw in a genuine piece will be extremely hard to remove owing to the thread not being tapered, and also because it will have rusted into the wood. A piece, therefore, that has screws with rusted heads, but which offer no resistance to the screwdriver, should be looked upon with suspicion.

Another test of the genuineness of a piece is in relation to handles. If the back plate of an original handle is removed from a genuine piece, the colour of the wood behind it is generally darker than the surrounding surface, where the wood or the polish will have been bleached by exposure. The faker, on the other hand, polishes the whole of his piece to an even tone, and then applies the handles, making no allowance for the surface to be darker where it is covered up.

SPURIOUS CARVING.

With regard to the decoration of plain pieces with spurious carving, not nearly so much of this has been done by the faker within recent years as in the past. A favourite piece on which to carry out this deception is the plain mahogany tripod table, of which many thousands have survived, and which specially lends itself to being so treated. The faker always chooses one that has bold legs of stoutish dimensions, in which there is enough material from which to carve the ornament. His difficulty is to find a tripod which has sufficient breadth in the foot for the carving of the claw and ball, as the majority of plain tripods are not wide enough in this respect to permit this *motif* being done in a bold manner typical of the good eighteenth century example. The result is that many of these carved-up tables have a narrow claw and ball of pinched appearance. In many cases the ball is omitted altogether, and the foot is formed of a claw only. Sometimes the foot of the original tripod is made to form the ball, and the claws are carved separately and glued on afterwards. To detect such a foot, a close examination should be made to see whether the grain of the wood forming the claw runs the same way as the grain forming the ball, which, of course, it would naturally do in an original table, when the claw and the ball were invariably carved out of the same piece. A familiarity with the contour of a genuine carved tripod leg will nearly always enable the collector to detect the carved-up example, which, in the process of being carved, will have lost its graceful curve and will, in consequence, look thin and ill-formed.

The tops of these tables are to-day receiving the attention of the faker, especially those with the pie-crust edge, which have risen considerably in value within recent years. This is due to the constant demand for pie-crust tops for genuine tripod tables, the original tops of which have been lost. The faker, therefore, supplies the demand by making spurious examples which he usually carves out of the plain tops belonging to plain tables. Sometimes he will make a top with elaborately carved decoration, formed of shells and acanthus foliage, in imitation of examples, figs. 185 and 189. A good test to prove the genuineness of a circular top is to see whether there is any variation in the measurements of the diameter, with the grain and across it. In a genuine top, the measurement with the grain should be anything from ⅛ of an inch to ½ an inch more than that across ; the reason being that the wood of an old top will have shrunk across the grain and not the way of it. In decorating an old plain top with a pie-crust edge, the top will first of all be turned on a lathe to reduce its thickness while leaving an outer rim out of which to carve the pie-crust edge. This process will make it a true circle again.

One of the differences between the genuine and the spurious piece lies in the arrises or edges, which should be felt to ascertain whether they are sharp, or worn and rounded. In an old piece, edges which are exposed, like those of a table top, or the edges of the sides of a bookcase, will have become rounded by the wood having been worn by polishing and rubbing, and by being bruised by objects coming into contact with them. In an unexposed or inaccessible position, an edge will be sharp. For instance, the back edge of the square leg of a table or chair will be much sharper than the other more exposed edges. It will also be sharper at the top of the leg than at the bottom, as this is the least exposed part. The edge of a moulding underneath a table top, which is protected by the overhang of the top, will be quite sharp. The same also applies to the mouldings of a cornice.

The faker will round the sharp edges of his pieces with a bone, but he does not make due allowance for the difference between those parts that are exposed, and those that are not. He may sometimes, by mistake, overlook an edge, but generally all the edges will be worn to a uniform evenness, very unlike the soft rounded edges of the genuine piece, caused by the accidental bruising and domestic polishing of a century and a half or more of use.

Wear also affects carving. The carved front edge of the top of a mahogany writing table will have the ornament worn and rounded through being rubbed when the table is in use, but on the sides near the back the carving will be as sharp as when it was originally executed. Very often the carved ornament on the end of the arms of both walnut and mahogany chairs will have distinct signs of being worn away through constant handling for generations. The same also applies to the cresting on the back of a chair, which will be handled almost every time it is moved. Walnut chairs will show much more wear on the carving than those made of hard Cuban mahogany. Dining-room chairs, however, made of the soft Honduras mahogany, will have the carving worn and rounded, especially on the knees of the cabriole legs, owing to those parts rubbing and knocking against each other when the chairs are in use. Sets of walnut chairs will also have suffered bruising and damage to the carving in the same way.

The faker will wear down the sharp edges of his carving—usually with a burnishing chain—but in the majority of cases he overdoes the worn appearance by not making allowance for the carving on the cresting and arms of a chair being more worn than that on the splat. It is easy for him to give a worn rounded effect to the carving, and therefore he treats it all mechanically in the same even manner, ignoring the fact that some parts may be as sharp as when they were originally carved, and others much worn through constant handling.

FAKED CHAIRS, "LOVE SEATS," STOOLS AND SETTEES.

The faker has ceased to make the over-elaborate examples of mahogany chairs, stools and settees with lion masks and eagle heads to which he was so partial about fifteen to twenty years ago. His attitude towards these articles to-day has undergone a change; instead of making a piece of new construction out of old wood, he finds it better and safer to alter and remake old chairs and stools into more valuable specimens. For example, an upholstered backed "love seat," which is like a small couch without a centre leg, is a very saleable and much sought after piece to-day. In order to make this piece, he uses the four legs of a single chair. The only new parts that are visible, therefore, are the four seat rails, the framework of the back and arms being hidden under the upholstery. This reconstruction converts a single mahogany chair which, if it has an upholstered back, is worth perhaps about £50, into a piece that is worth £200. A "love seat" made from a chair with walnut legs will show an even greater appreciation.

To overcome the difficulty of the exposed seat rails which, in the original piece, would be made of beech, the beech rails from a four-post bed are used. Such a bed, if it is an early nineteenth century example with coarsely turned mahogany posts, can be bought at a very low price. These bed-rails, which will be unpolished, will have the dry mature surface of age, and this surface will be left on the underneath and the inside of the seat rail. The freshly cut surface will be on the outside and on the top of the rail, which will be covered by upholstery. Sometimes, in order to overcome the difficulty of faking the seat rails, they are painted, as it is easier to give an appearance of age to a painted surface than to a wooden one. This is always a very suspicious feature, as no old chair would ever have been treated originally in such a manner. Familiarity with the appearance of the mature and dry surface of beech after it has been exposed to the atmosphere for a long period is a valuable asset in the detection of the spurious chair. For the framework of the back and arms, the faker will generally use modern beech, and will not even take the trouble to fake it, as, being covered up, it is improbable that it will ever be seen by the intending purchaser.

The winged arm-chair is another piece which is very saleable to-day. The difficulty for the faker in this case is that the legs of such a chair are shorter than those of an ordinary one, and, in consequence, he is unable to make this reconstruction correctly, unless he finds a chair with shorter legs than is usual. Sometimes, however, he will make a winged chair with tall legs, and such an example must always be viewed with misgiving. In order to obtain a supply of chair legs, the faker uses those that have been converted into stools, which was a favourite trick about twenty years ago, when a pair of single chairs were worth less than a stool. This resulted in many stools being made with cabriole legs which originally formed the front legs of a pair of chairs. Such stools can always be recognised from the fact that a chair leg will not have the top of the leg made at right angles, but at an acute angle, as the back of a chair is narrower than the front. Fashion having decreed that a pair of chairs or " love seats " with cabriole legs is worth more than one stool, these stools are now being converted back to their original state.

A chair with cabriole legs is worth considerably more than a chair with straight legs. Therefore, the faker will use a pair of cabriole chair legs, which he takes from a made-up stool, and fit them to a chair with straight legs. Such a chair must, of course, have an upholstered-over seat rail (fig. 169) and not a wooden seat rail with a drop-in seat (fig. 163). The difficulty about this reconstruction is that a straight-legged chair usually has stretchers, which a cabriole-legged chair does not. The faker, therefore, will have to hide the marks where the stretcher was tenoned into the back leg. Sometimes he will do this by covering the mark by veneering the inside face of the back leg. Very careful examination will have to be made before this will be discovered.

Chairs, " love seats " and couches with upholstered backs should have the upholstery removed to disclose the outer surface of the seat rails, to see whether they have been freshly cut*. Unless collectors and dealers will insist on this being done before purchasing, the faker will carry on his trade with regard to these articles with impunity.

---

* Particular note should be taken of the number of tack holes in the seat rail, as the upholstered-over seat of an old chair may have been recovered ten or fifteen times, with the result that the rail will be riddled with holes. There are exceptional cases where a chair will have its original upholstering which, if it is of some hard-wearing material such as needlework, is not improbable. Conversely, a chair that is supposed to have its original needlework covering, should not show signs in the frame work of having been upholstered many times, or more often than is consistent with the covering having been removed for the purpose of cleaning and restoring. The faker will often drive numbers of tacks into the seat rail of his spurious chair and extract them again so as to add a convincing detail for the benefit of the intending purchaser of the genuineness of the piece. It is essential for him to do this when he makes the seat rails out of bed rails, as already explained.

The early eighteenth century couch with upholstered back and arms, and cabriole legs of walnut, is an extremely saleable piece to-day. For the faker, however, it is a rather difficult piece to make, as, not only are the legs short in comparison with those of a chair, but the genuine examples invariably have a centre leg, and, if he makes such a settee from chair legs, he has either to omit the centre leg altogether or make a new one. Either alternative should arouse the suspicion of a purchaser.

Within recent years, dining room chairs with upholstered backs have become much in demand. This has resulted in sets of mahogany chairs with plain backs being converted into those of the upholstered back type. The partial removal of the upholstery from the back will soon disclose the freshly cut wood of the new framework.

As a test of the genuineness of the legs of chairs, the surface should be examined for scratches and marks, as the stretchers and legs of a genuine chair will invariably have their surfaces much damaged in this respect, owing to the kicks and knocks they will have received.

The bottom of the foot of a chair or table will be found in many spurious examples with the surface of the wood roughened and damaged, so as to give it an appearance of age. The faker in this respect generally overdoes this damaged appearance, as the characteristic of a genuine example is that the wood is usually smooth. Sometimes, in the case of light pieces that are often moved about, such as chairs and small tables, the surface will have acquired a slight polish caused by friction with the carpet.

Owing to the fact that a set of six chairs is considerably more valuable than a set of four, the faker often employs the following ingenious method of completing a set. For instance, if he requires two more chairs to make up a set of six, and makes two entirely new chairs, the difference between these and the old ones will be at once apparent. He therefore takes the four original chairs to pieces, and, having made the necessary members required for two new ones, he then assembles the six chairs and interposes the new parts with the old in each chair. The result is that every chair will have a new member, either a leg, a cresting, or a splat. Intermingling the old and the new parts in each chair makes it far more difficult for the fraud to be detected, especially as the faker is able to make his copy far more accurate by having the original member on the bench by his side.

An old trick that is still pursued to-day is the conversion of a single chair into an arm-chair, the single chair being worth a quarter or a third of the latter. The type of chair that the faker usually employs to-day for this purpose is the early eighteenth century single walnut chair with cabriole legs. The difference between the colour and the polish of the new arms and those of the rest of the chair is a guide to detection, in addition to which a single chair will be of narrower dimensions than the arm-chair. The trained eye can always detect the addition of arms to a single chair, as they will appear to be extraneous to it and destructive of its design.

The collector, in buying sets of chairs, should be careful to examine the arm-chairs, as they will often be modern, owing possibly to some previous purchaser of a set of six chairs, some fifteen or twenty years ago, having had two new arm-chairs made to complete the set.   Such arm-chairs, made without any intention to defraud, will now be difficult to detect after so long a period of domestic usage.

A number of spurious upholstered-backed chairs have been made recently with the arms and legs of chestnut.   The faker finds that such a wood more readily acquires an appearance of age when polished than walnut, which is partly due to its rougher texture.

FIG. 220.—INTERIOR OF A FAKED DRAWER MADE FROM OLD WOOD, WITH WORM HOLES CUT THROUGH.

A test to determine whether a chair is of new construction or not is to see if it feels rigid ; in other words, a modern chair will have the mortise and tenon joints which hold together the legs, stretchers and seat rail, tight and close fitting, and, consequently, when the chair is moved or lifted, it will have no " give " in any of its members.   If, on the contrary, it is an old chair, the joints will be looser owing to the shrinkage of the wood, and will therefore lack this rigidity and will yield under pressure.   It is possible, however, for an old chair to have this rigidity, because it may have been taken to pieces and repaired, and, when reassembled, all the joints will have been made tight and close-fitting again. The same test is also applicable to small tables.

WORM HOLES.

Worm holes are an undoubted sign of age to many people.   This is a fallacy that the faker turns to good account.   He does not, however, produce artificial worm holes such as in the past he is said to have done with the aid of a shot gun.   When he wishes to do so, he produces worm holes in a very much more realistic manner.   For example, if he wants worm holes in the beech seat rail of a chair, he will tie on to the rail a piece of old worm-eaten beech, and then place the chair in a dark room.   If the wood of the seat rail is dry and well seasoned, the worm from the old wood will start to burrow into it in the course of three or four months.   Sometimes, in using old timber, the faker, in cutting a plank, will expose the tunnelling of the worm, which will in consequence appear on the surface. Naturally, no worm works on the surface in this manner, and, therefore, wood which discloses worm holes that have been cut through shows that it is old wood that has been used in making a new piece (fig. 220). The old cabinet-maker would never have used a worm-eaten piece of wood even for his cheapest quality furniture. A piece, therefore, with the worm tunnelling cut through should always be viewed with suspicion. The soft wood carcasing of veneered pieces will often exhibit the worm holes on the surface in this manner when the veneer is stripped, as the worm burrows in the carcase wood just under the veneer.

Old veneer will also often exhibit similar worm holes on the surface. The presence of veneer worm-marked in this way usually denotes that the piece is spurious, the veneer having been taken from an old example and used again ; for, in the process of being relaid and repolished, the tunnelling of the worm, originally on the underneath side only, has gone right through the thickness of the veneer.

GENERAL REMARKS ON FAKING.

The instances that have been given in this chapter of the pieces which the faker alters and adapts, and the pieces of new construction which he makes from old wood, have not been singled out as examples against which the collector should be specially on his guard, as there remain any number of pieces, to which it has been impossible to make specific reference, which he treats in a similar manner. The real reason for selecting these particular examples is that they admirably serve to illustrate the faker's craft, and so give the reader an idea of how he works. Perhaps, in the next few years, the faker will have invented entirely new and improved methods of faking, and will be imitating whatever pieces may, at some future date, be in demand. To follow the latest machinations of the faker, it is necessary to keep up with his methods and to be constantly studying them.

An economic disadvantage with which the faker has to contend is that he cannot afford to give too much time to labour, as it will make his pieces so costly that no profit will accrue to him. At the present moment, however, he is still reaping a rich harvest because there is no necessity for him to reproduce in his work fine quality craftsmanship, since craftsmanship is seldom understood by the present-day collector. Quality of craftsmanship refers to constructional work such as dovetailing and the fitting of drawer bottoms, carving, the execution of cross-grained mouldings, the laying of cross-banded edgings and herring-bone inlay, and the matching of veneers. The study of how this work was carried out on the old examples will reveal how poor in quality the imitations of the faker really are. The mistake the faker makes to-day is to neglect quality of workmanship in order to concentrate on obtaining fictitious signs of age. Another handicap with which the faker has to contend is the difficulty of obtaining finely figured woods of the same high quality as the old varieties used. Knowledge of woods is a great asset for the collector to possess, and a great help in detecting a spurious piece. A careful analysis of an old piece of high quality will show that many different woods can be used in one piece. For example, a cabinet may have small panels of yew or amboyna with cross-grained mouldings of olive, while the main portions of the carcase are veneered with walnut. An unobservant collector would not notice such refinements as the use of choice woods of this description. He is, therefore, unlikely to detect their absence in the faker's imitation. An indication of economy of labour and consequent loss in quality of craftsmanship is the absence of the cross-banded cock bead, which is not used by the faker as it would involve too much labour.

It is this question of knowledge of and familiarity with craftsmanship and material which ultimately will defeat the faker. The more the collector and dealer know about these subjects, the more difficult and expensive will the faker's work become, until, finally, he will be driven out of business altogether. There is as much danger in the work the faker has done in the past as in what he is likely to do in the future, since, unquestionably, many of his pieces, which have changed hands many times, are considered by their present owners to be genuine period examples. It is a pity that faked furniture cannot be publicly branded as spurious, so that it will cease to deceive, in the same way that silver with fraudulent assay marks is confiscated. Such a procedure might make serious inroads on many a private collection and museum, but, if it resulted in the proper understanding of old English furniture, or, for that matter, of foreign furniture as well—as the faker is not peculiar to England—it would be of the utmost value to the student and collector of the future. It would spare the former the farce of examining and appraising the faker's work, and the latter his money in purchasing spurious pieces which one day, sooner or later, are sure to be discovered, when knowledge of old furniture is more widely possessed.

It is absurd to belittle the work of the faker, as, even after eliminating his ordinary commercial imitations, which are so palpable that they would not take in anyone with the smallest knowledge, there is still in existence a vast quantity of reconstructed pieces of furniture, of pieces of entirely new construction made of old wood, and of plain pieces made into ornamented examples by carving and inlay, masquerading as genuine, and, as time goes on and they continue to escape detection, becoming more and more believed in as such.

THE RESTORATION OF OLD PIECES.

A piece that has had extensive restorations carried out is naturally not so valuable as one that is in a mint state. It is always desirable, therefore, to know the amount of restoration that a piece has been subjected to. In order to do this, examination in a strong light is essential, so as to be able to detect the different colours of the wood in the restored and the original parts, and the difference in the polish. How much restoration depreciates the value of a piece depends, first, upon the amount that has been done and the importance of the parts restored, and, secondly, upon the rarity of the piece. A form of restoration that does not affect the value is the replacing of missing pieces, such as cross-grained mouldings, small portions of veneer, cock beads to drawers and small wings to legs which, being made apart from the leg, often drop off in the course of time. A broken arm or leg depreciates the value to a certain extent, as the defect, even when carefully restored, is unsightly and the structure of the piece is weakened. A restoration that does materially affect the value of a piece is when a part is missing or so badly damaged that it has to be replaced : an example of this is a new arm or a new leg.　If the piece is not a very rare and valuable one, then the presence of a new arm or leg will depreciate its value considerably.　By this is meant that a plain mahogany chair with a new leg would not be considered worth buying by a collector, because he would have no difficulty in getting another of a similar type in a perfect state.　If, on the other hand, a very

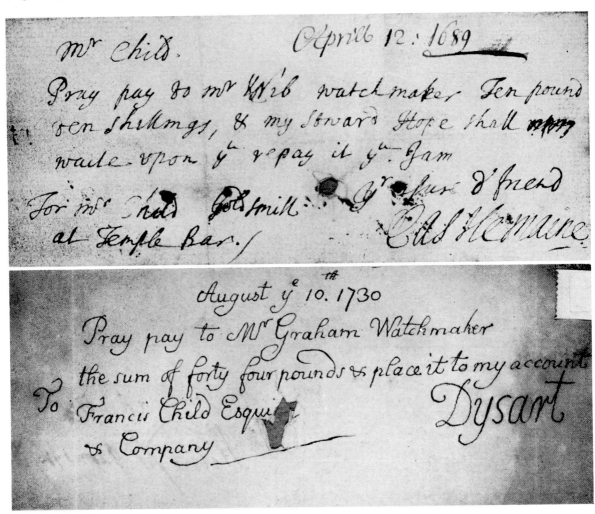

FIG. 221.—TWO CHEQUES, ONE TO MR. KNIBB, SIGNED BY THE EARL OF CASTLEMAINE, AND THE OTHER TO MR. GRAHAM, SIGNED BY THE EARL OF DYSART.　THESE ARE OF EXCEPTIONAL INTEREST, NOT ONLY BECAUSE THEY ARE PAYMENTS TO TWO FAMOUS CLOCKMAKERS, BUT ALSO BECAUSE ONE BEARS THE SIGNATURE OF THE HUSBAND OF THE BEAUTIFUL LADY CASTLEMAINE, MISTRESS OF CHARLES II.

important and rare chair had a new leg, then, because of its rarity, it would still be of interest, although, naturally, it would be worth more if all four legs were original.

More walnut pieces have been restored than mahogany.　This—as already explained on page 17—is due to the walnut furniture being veneered on a soft wood carcase, which attracts the worm, and to portions of the mouldings becoming loose and dropping off, as they were cross-grained.　Walnut chairs, especially, are defective, owing to the back legs becoming worm eaten, as these were more often made of beech than of walnut. If the back leg of a walnut chair gets riddled with worm, the only satisfactory way to restore it is by making a new one. Sometimes this new leg is spliced on to the side rail of the back where it joins the seat, but in other cases the side rail has also been renewed, the old veneer on the front face having been taken off and replaced.

The tops of walnut dressing tables, similar to examples illustrated (figs. 117 and 118), will sometimes have new veneer, either because the old veneer has broken away, generally through ill-treatment, or because sometimes the central panel of the veneer will have been removed and a leather top applied in its stead, to convert the table into a writing table. A new veneered top of this description will depreciate the value of the table by at least 30 per cent. or 40 per cent. The veneer on the top of a walnut card table will often be found to be new, and sometimes the back leg will be a modern restoration, as, owing to the original leg being hinged on to the frame so that it would pull out to support the flap, it was liable to get broken. The chest on stand often has the legs of the stand restored, especially the type of chest illustrated in fig. 31. The heavy weight of the upper part on the slender legs causes them to break, with the result that by far the greater number of these chests on stands have modern legs. This depreciates their value by at least 75 per cent., as the design of such a piece is more or less dependent on the stand. In these chests on stands, even when the legs are old, the flat veneered stretchers have very often been restored or entirely renewed. This also applies to the seventeenth century oblong table, which has similar stretchers. When stretchers of this type are restored they are usually made too thick, and are often veneered on the edges, because, if the restorer uses old deal for the foundation of his veneer, the edges will be freshly cut. In order to overcome the difficulty of faking the unpolished surface of this deal edge, he will hide it by veneer, which he then polishes. On original stretchers, the edges will seldom be found veneered.

A *motif* of design which sometimes denotes a restoration is the presence of a collar on a cabriole leg just above the claw-and-ball foot. A number of genuine chairs and settees have survived with this *motif* decorating the leg, but it is also sometimes employed as a means of hiding the join between the foot and the leg, when the former is a modern addition. The reason for a new foot to a leg is that the chair has been cut down to make it lower for some purpose, or because worm has attacked the foot and the wood has been eaten away. To detect whether this restoration has been carried out—which considerably depreciates the value of a piece—the back legs should be examined to see whether they have also had a piece added on, which will be easy to discern as it would be incorrect to fix a collar on a back leg, since no genuine example has survived with this feature. Sometimes, however, in order to overcome this difficulty, new back legs will have been fitted. Careful examination should also be made to see whether the grain of the wood is continuous above and below the collar. If it is so, it would point to the leg being made out of one piece of wood, which would denote that it was genuine. Also examine the profile of the leg to see whether the curve above and below the collar is continuous and in one line. To produce this is extremely difficult, as, if the new foot is the slightest fraction out, it will immediately show. This type of restoration is seldom found except on walnut pieces.

One point, with regard to restored parts, is that when they have been recently done it will often be hard to detect them except by very careful examination. In five or six years time, however, such parts—especially in walnut examples—will show up in contrast to the remainder of the piece, owing to the polish with which

FIG. 222.—DETAIL OF MIRROR, FIG. 224

they have been treated—in order to make them look like the original—altering in colour. This is due to the polish reacting to the acid with which the wood of the restored parts has been treated. It does not always occur, as it depends upon the skill of the restorer.

This question of restoration is an important one, as many pieces of furniture that are complete wrecks, with a large amount of the veneer missing and the cross-grained mouldings gone, in the hands of a careful restorer can be made to look in a perfect state to an inexperienced person. Naturally, to restore old furniture is the right thing to do, but it is essential that the missing portions should not only be of correct design, but that the original proportions of the piece should not be altered by the addition of the restored parts. In many cases this is where the restorer fails, as he will make the new legs of a chest on stand either too short or too high, so that the proportion of the entire piece will not be as satisfactory as it undoubtedly once was.

The reason why restoration has been commented on here is to show how it affects the value of furniture; therefore, every purchaser should always try to ascertain, to the best of his ability, the amount of restoration that has actually been carried out.

The collector's criterion of excellence should be the piece which, in addition to good design, is in its original condition, which means that its surface should not only possess the original polish, but also a patina acquired through the natural process of time. The far-sighted collector realises that a piece in this state is, artistically and commercially, worth far more than a piece which has been re-polished or over-restored.

The illustrations in this book are of pieces in their original condition, as none of them has been damaged by re-polishing or over-restoration.

T

FIG. 223.—MIRROR WITH CARVED GILT ENRICHMENTS AND MOULDINGS AND
THE FLAT SURFACES VENEERED WITH WALNUT.
CIRCA 1735.

FIG. 224.—MIRROR WITH GILT GESSO FRAME.   CIRCA 1735.
FOR DETAIL, SEE FIG. 222.

233

Fig. 225.—MIRROR WITH FRAME AND CRESTING OF GREEN AND GOLD VERRE
EGLOMISÉ   THE MOULDINGS TO HOOD AND FRAME ARE OF STAMPED
METAL GILT.   CIRCA 1695.
THIS MIRROR IS MOST PROBABLY OF CONTINENTAL PROVENANCE.

FIG. 226.—PIER GLASS WITH BEVELLED GLASS BORDERS AND
SHAPED GLASS HOOD.   CIRCA 1710.

235

FIG. 227.—PAIR OF PIER GLASSES WITH FRAMES OF SOFT WOOD DECORATED WITH BLACK AND GOLD LACQUER IN THE CHINESE TASTE. CIRCA 1720.
SUCH PAIRS OF TALL MIRRORS WERE DESIGNED TO HANG BETWEEN WINDOWS WITH SIDE-TABLES UNDERNEATH.

236

237

FIG. 228.—MIRROR WITH CARVED WALNUT MOULDINGS AND ENRICHMENTS AND THE FLAT SURFACES VENEERED WITH FINELY FIGURED WALNUT
THE MOULDINGS AND ENRICHMENTS OF THIS MIRROR BEING IN CARVED WALNUT MAKE IT A VERY UNUSUAL EXAMPLE.   CIRCA 1730.

FIG. 229.—WALNUT AND GILT MIRROR OF UNUSUALLY BOLD DESIGN.   CIRCA 1745.

FIG. 231.—MIRROR WITH FRAME AND HOOD DECORATED WITH SEAWEED MARQUETRY. CIRCA 1690.

FIG. 230.—MIRROR, ONE OF A PAIR, WITH CARVED WOOD AND GILT FRAME. CIRCA 1730.

238

FIG. 232 (LEFT).—MAHOGANY LONG-CASE CLOCK OF UNUSUAL DESIGN, WITH EIGHT-DAY MOVEMENT, BY JOHN
VALE, LONDON.   FOR DETAIL, SEE FIG. 237.   CIRCA 1735.
      THIS CLOCK WAS FORMERLY THE PROPERTY OF WILLIAM HOGARTH, AND WAS SOLD WITH HIS EFFECTS.

FIG. 233 (RIGHT).—PIER GLASS, ONE OF A PAIR, WITH BEVELLED GLASS BORDERS.   CIRCA 1700.

FIG. 234.—FIRE-SCREEN OF GILT GESSO WORK, WITH PANEL OF A DESIGN PAINTED ON CANVAS IN IMITATION OF TAPESTRY.
CIRCA 1715.

FOR DETAIL, SEE FIG. 2.

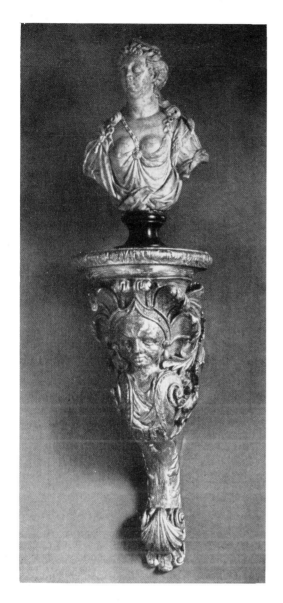

FIG. 235.—CARVED WOOD AND GILT BRACKET
ONE OF A PAIR.   CIRCA 1725.

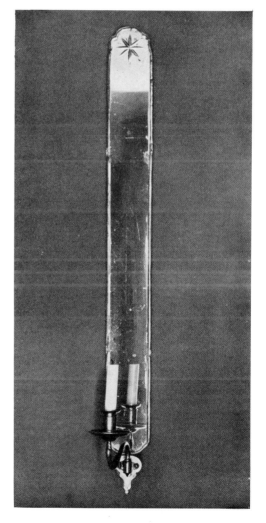

FIG. 236.—SCONCE WITH MIRROR BACK DESIGNED
TO FIT IN A CORNER.   ONE OF A SET OF FOUR.
CIRCA 1715.

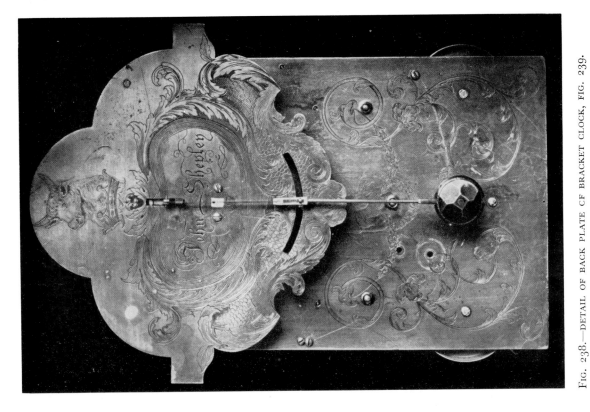

FIG. 238.—DETAIL OF BACK PLATE OF BRACKET CLOCK, FIG. 239.

242

FIG. 237.—DETAIL OF HOOD AND DIAL OF FIG. 232.

FIG. 239.—AN UNUSUAL WALNUT BRACKET CLOCK ON A WALNUT TABLE, WHICH WAS UNDOUBTEDLY MADE FOR IT. THE THREE-TRAIN CHIMING MOVEMENT IS BY JOHN SHEPLEY, STOCKPORT.   CIRCA 1740.
FOR DETAIL OF BACK PLATE, SEE FIG. 238.

243

FIG. 241.—SMALL BRACKET CLOCK WITH ARCHED TOP, IN ORMOLU MOUNTED SCAGLIOLA CASE. HEIGHT, 7 INCHES. MOVEMENT BY JAMES TREGENT. CIRCA 1780.

FIG. 240.—SMALL MAHOGANY BRACKET CLOCK WITH ARCHED TOP. MOVEMENT BY PAUL RIMBAULT, LONDON. HEIGHT OF CASE, 6½ INCHES. CIRCA 1785.

244

FIG. 242.—BRACKET CLOCK IN VENEERED KINGWOOD CASE.
MOVEMENT BY NATHANAEL HODGES.   CIRCA 685.

FIG. 243.—BRACKET CLOCK IN VENEERED PEARWOOD CASE, EBONISED, WITH
SILVER MOUNTS.   MOVEMENT BY THOMAS HERBERT.   CIRCA 1685.

245

FIG. 244.—BRACKET CLOCK IN VENEERED WALNUT CASE.
MOVEMENT BY JOSEPH WINDMILLS, LONDON.   CIRCA 1690.

FIG. 245.—DETAIL SHOWING ENGRAVED BACK PLATE.

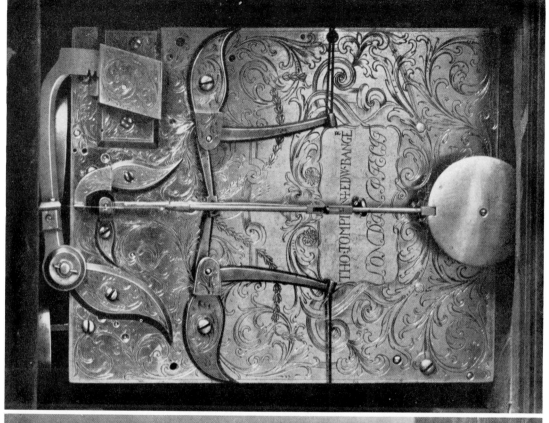

FIG. 247.—DETAIL SHOWING ENGRAVED BACK PLATE.

FIG. 246.—BRACKET CLOCK IN VENEERED PEARWOOD CASE, EBONISED.
MOVEMENT BY THO. TOMPION AND EDW. BANGER, LONDON.   CIRCA 1710.

247

FIG. 249.—BRACKET CLOCK IN VENEERED WALNUT CASE.
MOVEMENT BY JOHN KNIBB, OXFORD.   CIRCA 1690.

FIG. 248.—BRACKET CLOCK IN VENEERED TORTOISESHELL CASE.
1680.
MOVEMENT BY JOHANNES FROMANTEEL.

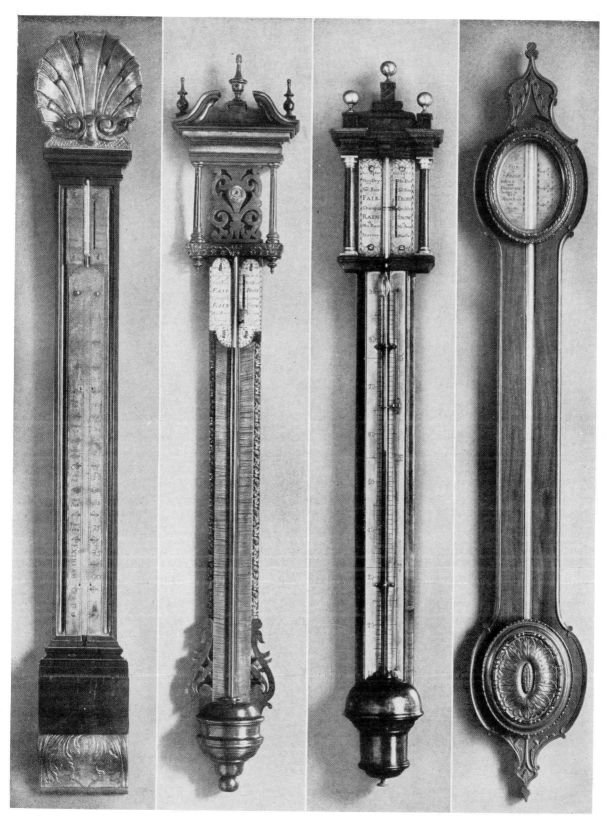

FIG. 250.—WALNUT AND
GILT WALL BAROMETER,
BY PAT SULIVAN, LONDON.
CIRCA 1740.

FIG. 251.—WALNUT AND
SYCAMORE WALL BARO-
METER.   CIRCA 1760.

FIG. 252.—WALNUT WALL
BAROMETER.   CIRCA 1740.

FIG. 253.—MAHOGANY WALL
BAROMETER.   CIRCA 1770.

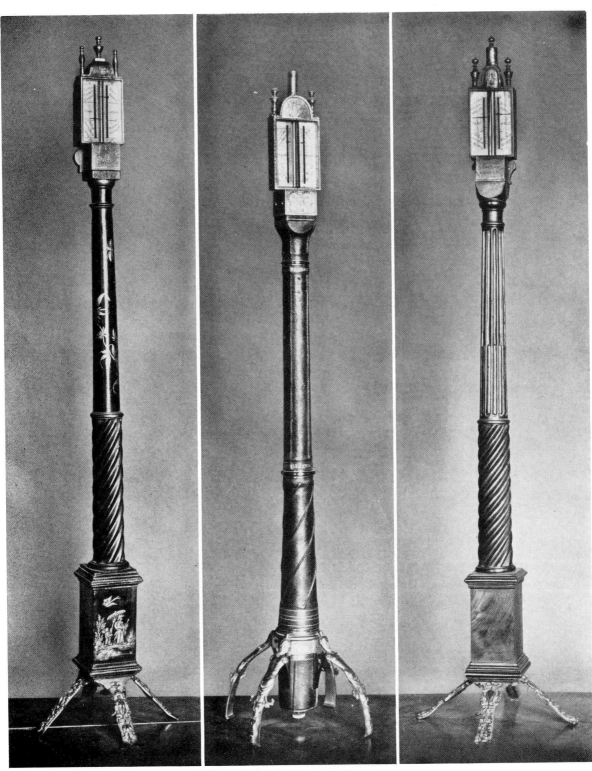

FIG. 254.—A PORTABLE BAROMETER
DECORATED IN BLACK AND GOLD
LACQUER.   CIRCA 1715.

FIG. 255.—A PORTABLE BAROMETER
WITH CASE COVERED IN SHARK-SKIN,
BY DANIEL QUARE, WITH ENGLISH AND
FRENCH TABLE.   CIRCA 1700.

FIG. 256.—A WALNUT PORTABLE
BAROMETER, BY DANIEL QUARE.
CIRCA 1710.

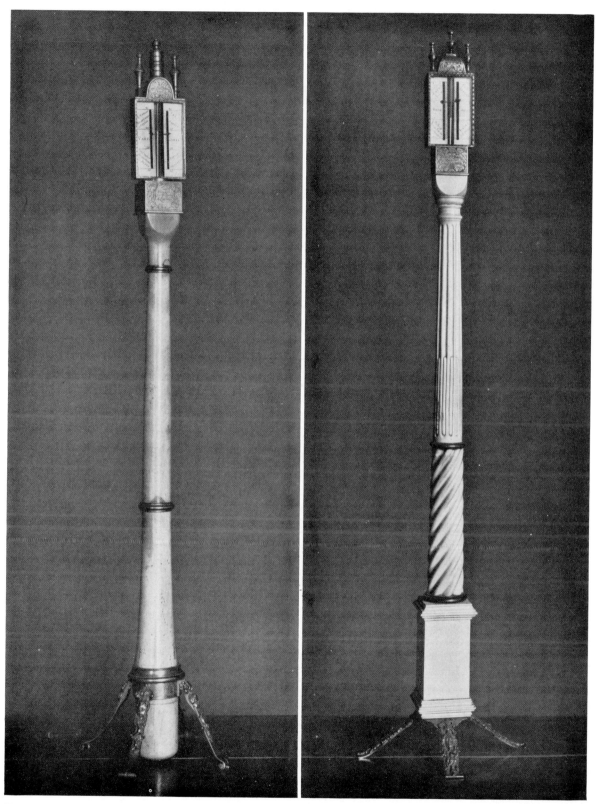

FIG. 257.—AN IVORY PORTABLE BAROMETER, BY DANIEL QUARE, WITH AN ENGLISH AND FRENCH TABLE.   CIRCA 1695.

FIG. 258.—AN IVORY PORTABLE BAROMETER, BY DANIEL QUARE.   CIRCA 1710.

251

FIG. 259.-WHEEL BAROMETER, BY GEORGE GRAHAM, IN VERY UNUSUAL PEARWOOD
EBONISED WALL-CASE.   HEIGHT, 43 IN.
CIRCA 1720.

INDEX TO LETTERPRESS

INDEX TO ILLUSTRATIONS